CHENGDU
TEAHOUSE

www.royalcollins.com

CHENGDU TEAHOUSE

Half of the City's Dwellers Are Tea Drinkers

He Xiaozhu

Translated by Feng Juan

RC

—— *Books Beyond Boundaries* ——

ROYAL COLLINS

Chengdu Teahouse
Half of the City's Dwellers Are Tea Drinkers

He Xiaozhu
Translated by Feng Juan

First published in 2023 by Royal Collins Publishing Group Inc.
Groupe Publication Royal Collins Inc.
BKM Royalcollins Publishers Private Limited

Headquarters: 550-555 boul. René-Lévesque O Montréal (Québec) H2Z1B1 Canada
India office: 805 Hemkunt House, 8th Floor, Rajendra Place, New Delhi 110008

ISBN: 978-1-4878-1156-3

To find out more about our publications, please visit www.royalcollins.com.

Contents

General Preface

What is Tianfu culture? Tianfu culture is the culture that emerged, developed, and flourished in the "Land of Abundance" (Land of Tianfu), centered on Chengdu or the West Sichuan Plain, which is, to a certain extent, the culture of Chengdu, the traditions of Chengdu, and the unique way of life of Chengdu formed over thousands of years. It is history, it is life, and it is every day. It is deeply imprinted in our memories, and it flows in our blood. It exists in places where we can see or cannot see, being a habit of thinking, or a way of behavior, or mood, an opinion, a hobby, or a kind of feature …

While researchers in the past have focused more on cities like Beijing and Shanghai that have undergone drastic changes in the modern era, I have always believed that Chengdu is more representative of Chinese cities because it is located inland and contains richer Chinese elements and preserves more traditional culture. Chengdu is a typical Chinese city, and such a city can represent many similar Chinese inland cities, showing us a different urban landscape from the coastal ones.

The richness of the Chengdu Plain has provided a guarantee for the development of Chengdu's urban economy and shaped the unique material culture of Tianfu. The historical origin of Tianfu culture can be traced back to ancient Shu, an ancient seigneur kingdom in the pre-Qin period. Dujiangyan is an important source of Tianfu culture, fostering its innovative spirit, laying the material foundation of Tianfu culture, developing rice agriculture in the West Sichuan Plain, and providing a solid material foundation for the "Land of Abundance" for more than 2,000 years, as well as promoting the organic combination of nature and humanity, farming and urban civilizations, and native and foreign cultures.

The Tianfu culture is rooted in the West Sichuan Plain and integrated into people's way of life with idyllic gardens, food, poetry, music, and recreation. The West Sichuan Plain has a very deep humanistic deposit, which has bred many outstanding talents in various fields, including literature, politics, military, science and technology, and business. It has injected new vitality into the Tianfu culture and promoted its flourishing. At the same time, the Tianfu culture is constantly intermingling with other cultures, absorbing the essence of other cultures and making its unique contribution to Chinese culture.

The reason for the prosperity of Tianfu culture is that the West Sichuan Plain is blessed with unique conditions such as the environment, climate, products, and transportation, and we need to fully understand and cherish these factors. In today's world, almost the cities that are better built and developed have an organic and reasonable combination of traditional culture and modern civilization, where the growth of the material economy and spiritual culture go hand in hand.

To understand a city's yesterday is to understand the city's today better; to understand a city's today is to build and create a better future for the city. In this famous Chinese historical and cultural city, many historical and cultural sites have been destroyed or even disappeared with the changing times, so protecting the memory of Tianfu culture is essential. Culture is the unique imprint of a city that can showcase the true, three-dimensional, and comprehensive image of a city.

We can get to know a city from many perspectives, with different materials, and by focusing on different topics. Chengdu Times Publishing House has selected ten of the more than seventy books on Tianfu culture published over the years and reprinted them as the Tianfu Culture City Series. These books cover ancient civilization, cultural relics and archaeology, literature and poetry, and daily life in the land of Tianfu, basically covering all aspects of Tianfu culture from ancient times to the present day.

I think this is a very good way of thinking and has created excellent conditions for these books to receive renewed attention. The introduction and study of Shu civilization, Tianfu culture, and the city of Chengdu provided by this set of books is beneficial to our understanding of the city and its culture, and makes a significant contribution to the study of the city. In the writing of this set of books, the local scholars of Chengdu have played a major role, tirelessly collecting information, carrying out fieldwork, painstaking researching, and diligent writing to explore and understand the city's past, presenting us with the city's colorful culture and history, and providing very valuable information and spiritual food for readers concerned with Tianfu culture.

WANG DI

July 2, 2021

1

Legends

According to *An Overview of Chengdu*: in the late Qing Dynasty (AD 1636–1912), there were 516 streets and alleys in Chengdu, and almost every street was dotted with teahouses which amounted to 454 teahouses.

Shu people have been drinking tea since ancient times. As early as 59 BC, Wang Bao of the Zizhong people recorded in *Tong Yue* (an agreement between the host and the servant) that a widow in Western Shu called Yang Hui brewed tea at home: "There were guests visiting, so she carried a pot to buy wine … They brewed tea, poured tea in cups, covered them after drinking." It is said that this is the earliest and clearest record of the Shu people drinking tea.

Legend has it that men in Chengdu do not do anything but just stay in the teahouse, chatting all day long.

Legend has it that the world's first-ever teahouse was opened in Chengdu at least a thousand years ago.

Legend has it that after Li Bing and his son repaired the Dujiangyan, the Chengdu Plain was flood-free and drought-free. The desires could be easily satisfied. People sowed in spring and harvested a houseful of food in autumn. People have had nothing to do since then, with a lot of time with nowhere to spend it.

The Jinjiang River flowing through the gallery bridge of Baihuatan Park is the mother river that has nourished the teahouses in Chengdu.

They were invited up to the mountains to pick a kind of tree leaf, knead them, and then soak them in water to drink from morning to night. Over time, they felt it boring to drink alone at home, so they began to gather together to drink. For example, under the shade of a tree, along the street, or on the river dam, everyone chatted idly while drinking tea with a tea bowl in his hands, squatting or sitting on the ground. Time was killed very easily. Some intelligent people found that this was a side business that could also earn money without sowing the seeds. They then built a shed and a stove and set up a square table and bamboo chairs, so that people could sit comfortably without being exposed to the sun and rain. They even didn't need to take pains to pick leaves and boil water but to prepare a few pieces of silver in the sleeve or belt. Someone would make tea for them, and even pound their back, rub their shoulders, and clean their ears, as well as cut hair or fingernails for them. How about being hungry? You don't even have to go home and bother to lift your butt from the chair, and just yell, "Hi, a bowl of wonton please, with spicy sauce," so a bowl of wonton with spicy sauce would be brought to your hands.

Legend has it that the first person who built a shed to sell tea was a widow. Widows, of course, have less trouble than the average woman. They have more extra time so as to share some with others.

Legend has it that people in Chengdu go to the teahouse not mainly for tea, but to kill time. To feel the time flies fast, and so fast that people do not notice the traces of its speed, there is nothing better than to talk more, talk without stopping. The chatting content may cover topics from the sky to the earth, from the past to the present, and even gossip about various people, all of which are called the "Longmen Zhen." At first, people talked with each other in a mess. Then, suddenly one day, all the people in the teahouse stayed quiet, and only a person was still there talking—about history, myths, street affairs, and strange and interesting stories in society. Thus, there appeared a seat for the storyteller. As soon as people came to the teahouse, they would push that talkative person to the seat and say: "You are good at storytelling. We will listen to your story today exclusively." When a person talks alone, it's more easily for him to feel thirsty than the others. So, the teahouse owner would frequently offer him tea and say, "This is free." What's more, the owner felt that there were really many more bowls of tea sold every day than before with this talkative person sitting there talking and talking, so he said to that storyteller: "Sir, you moisten your throat and continue to talk, the more, the better. If a bowl of tea was sold out, I would give you a penny, so that your energy will not be wasted for nothing." As soon as the man heard it, he thought it was great. Instead of holding the words in the stomach, it's better to spit them out, and there is money to be earned. Well, let's put it away. Since the storyteller started his business, naturally there should be something different. He had to make some preparation and put on some fancy styles, for example, holding a folding fan or something in his hand. When the story came to a critical juncture, he would stop and open the folding fan with the sound of clatter and shake unhurriedly. In this way, he could take the opportunity to take a break, drink tea to moisten the throat, and also tantalize the tea drinkers' appetite for the following plot as well. As a result, Chengdu teahouses began to have a saying of "enjoy storytelling while drinking tea," that is, tea drinkers go to the teahouses and drink tea while listening to a professional storyteller talking "Longmen Zhen." Under such circumstances, time flies so fast that people nearly forget the existence of time.

However, gradually, people are not satisfied with simply listening to the storytelling again. One day, a few people brought a set of gongs and drums and a huqin into the teahouse, "Let's sing a few songs," they said. Urged by the drumbeat, chased by the gongs and cymbals, plus with the accompaniment of the huqin, they sit in a circle, pulling their voices to climb a slope and cross a river, attracting bursts of applause from the tea drinkers. Thus, there was one more way to kill time: "Come on, let's go to the teahouse of Wan Happiness to listen to Ran Mazi and his men playing the percussion drums."

Such names as Wan Happiness and Ran Mazi are, of course, ones that are made up, but in the past and past, in the Chengdu plain, whether it's in the courtyard or in the city, teahouses like Wan Happiness where people "enjoy storytelling while drinking tea" and "play gongs and drums" can be realized and can be said to be innumerable. And tea drinkers like Ran Mazi, who earned some fame, counted many naturally. No wonder from very early on, people have concluded that Chengdu has "three manys," that is, many teahouses, many toilets, and many idle people.

Legend has it that more than 100 years ago, there was a famous idler in Huayang County, Chengdu, named Su Laosan. When he was born, he babbled in the hustle and bustle of the teahouse and grew up crawling and fighting among the tables and benches. Because his family lived upstairs in a teahouse; to be precise, his father, Su Gunlong, nicknamed "Humpback Su," ran a teahouse here. Don't think that the son of the teahouse owner is some kind of rich boy. Yes, Su's family background was just average. In Chengdu's small streets and alleys, setting up a dozen or 20 tables and running such a teahouse does not require much money, or even no money. If there were a teahouse, there would be a toilet. The nightman would come and pay the deposit first, and then all the feces from the toilets attached to the teahouse belonged to him. There were also fortune-tellers, ear-pickers, sellers of melon seeds, peanuts, and tobacco, as well as barbers and other craftsmen, who also depended on the teahouse to make a living. They also had to pay a deposit (similar to the current entrance fee), and only after the teahouse opened could they enter the venue and have a booth of their own. So, after you receive the deposit, you could rent a house, buy the tables and chairs, build a stove, bring water from the river, and start a bustling business. However, there was usually one or even several such teahouses in your street and alley, and competition was inevitable. Therefore, the profit earned by the teahouse was not very proportional to the prosperity of the teahouse industry. After deducting the salaries paid to the cook, the servant, and the handyman, the monthly income was only enough for a family's daily expenses. That's it.

Legend has it that Su Laosan did not inherit his father's business. The grown-up Su Laosan did not open a teahouse as his father did, but soaked in the teahouse every day. Moreover, he also thought that Huayang's world was too small and felt like a duck in water only when he was in a teahouse in Chengdu. At that time, at least half of the servers of teahouses in Chengdu knew this Uncle Su. "Uncle Su, good morning." When he walked into a certain teahouse, a waiter with a copper pot in his hand greeted him so loudly.

A view of the tea garden in Daci Temple in the past: the tea drinkers were seated among the shade of trees, calligraphy and painting. No wonder the poet Liushahe had a special liking for this place. (The picture was provided by Jiang Hai, a friend of mine.)

The tea garden in Daci Temple in the rain in the past. (The picture was provided by Jiang Hai, a friend of mine.)

"Morning, morning." Su Laosan waved his hand and found his regular seat. At this time, a tea drinker next to him would greet the waiter: "I will pay for the tea for Uncle Su." This was called "calling for the tea money." "Calling for the tea money" means that when you enter the teahouse, the acquaintance who arrived before you will shout, "I will pay for the tea for Uncle XX." The more people call for tea money for you, the greater your face is, which shows that you have many friends and enjoy popularity and prestige. Su Laosan was such an uncle. When he walked into any teahouse, many people were calling for tea money for him. Su Laosan bowed his hands and said, "Thank you, thank you," or "Next time, next time."

How could Su Laosan be so great? He did not work in the government nor in the business circle, so he can be said to be jobless. He could not even read a few words. Growing up with his father in the teahouse, the knowledge he gained was either from the storyteller, from the tea guests' chatting, or from what he saw—look at the appearances of all beings to understand the ordinary things on earth. This was the so-called "being unconsciously influenced by what one constantly hears or sees." Su Laosan understood the world clearly. So, he did not go to the hard work of seeking any fame, but decided to be an idler in the teahouse. In fact, the "idler" was not idle. He did nothing all day long but drank tea and bubble in the teahouse. Unlike those craftsmen who cut hair and did ear-cleansing for people in the teahouse, however, drinking tea and talking was his work, his occupation, and his business. Su Laosan, Uncle Su, also had a nickname called "Su Half City," that is, he dared not say he knew all the celebrities in Chengdu, but knew at least half of them. His business was people. This was not about the trader in human beings, but as a mediator. For example, if Zhang San wanted to meet Li Si, he would ask for Su Half City to serve as a bridge; if the Xie's wanted to sell something to the Wang's, they asked Su Laosan for help as well; if the East's argued with the West's, they called Uncle Su to mediate. This was called "mediation while drinking tea." So, Su Laosan was busy with his lips. "Well, well, my mouth is dry. Let's settle the matter like this. You, you, and you, all listen to …" In this way, Uncle Su, Su Laosan, lived his life and passed his days.

About "mediation while drinking tea," Mr. Li Jieren once wrote in his novel *Before the Storm*: "If you had a quarrel with someone, and you want to fight for face to judge who is right and who is wrong, but do not like to be engaged in a lawsuit, then you can invite some people to meet at a teahouse, naturally, the more, the better. It's the same with your opponent too. If one side is more powerful while the other side is gentler, it is effortless to judge and solve the issue. Like this, both sides quarrel loudly for a while, and the so-called intermediary mediates for a while, then tell off the gentle side for minutes. Even if the gentle side lost, no apologies are needed. They only need to pay for a few or a dozen tables of the two sides, and the matter could be called solved."*

Legend has it that after the Republic of China, the authorities were determined to eradicate bad habits, and strengthen the legal system. Thus, it forbade "mediation while drinking tea" in the teahouse, and advocated going to court to solve matters. It undoubtedly cut off half of Su Laosan's fortune. And teahouse owners were not happy with this practice too, because the teahouse's social status would be shaken, not to mention that their business

---

*Quoted from the third edition of *Before the Storm* published by Sichuan Literature and Art Publishing House in August 2020.

LEFT A monk in Daci Temple.

ABOVE The sky shot from a low angle on the Jiuyan Bridge. Such blue sky and white clouds are rare in Chengdu. Such a day is called "tea drinking day" by the Chengdu people.

would also be affected without the social activity "mediation while drinking tea." Therefore, they went to the new government with a joint petition, asking them not to interfere too much with teahouse customs.

Legend has it that the matter was left unresolved. The so-called "unresolved" meant that the ban was still there, and "mediation while drinking tea" was still there, too, because many matters could not be explained clearly in court, but could be solved in the teahouse.

The legendary Chengdu teahouse was such a place where people from all walks of life converged. Teahouses are on all corners of the country. Especially the legend of the teahouse in the early Republic of China was more suitable for writing novels and making them into movies. The famous "pier" organized by the Sichuan Pao Ge association was often set in these small and large teahouses. This secret organization was a bit "revolutionary" in its early years when it was founded to "fight against the Qing Dynasty and restore the Ming Dynasty (AD 1368–1644)," but evolved into a gangsterdom after the establishment of the Republic of China. Therefore, in those turbulent times, the gangsterdom's trades of guns and opium were often carried out in the teahouses. In addition, the teahouse also played the role of "helping with an emergency." All the people who had no way out of life could often get financial assistance if they went to the teahouse to ask for help. Legend has it that the people who went to the teahouse for help were some of the "criminal" people, so their asking for help also carried a certain degree of secrecy. Generally, the help-seeker pretended to drink tea in the teahouse as if nothing had happened. When the teahouse attendant served the tea guest water for a second time, they found that the teacup lid could not be found, and he might be a little alarmed at the tea guest. Sure enough, this disguiser uncovered the straw hat on the table, revealing the teacup lid that he had previously hidden. This is a signal, an argot, or called "qie kou." When the teahouse attendant saw this, he immediately understood and gave an argot response, inviting guests to talk in the backyard. The person who conversed with the guest was the teahouse owner. After he asked the reason, he would give some money to the guest to ease the situation on the one hand, and on the other, to point a way out for him. The so-called "way" is to introduce him to another "pier" to work together. The generous teahouse owner, in fact, was a Pao Ge here who had some rights. However, there were also such cases where the teahouse attendant talked with the help-seeker for a while, but suddenly poured out the tea and walked away. It indicated that the "pier" for some reason, did not want to interfere in such matters, and requested the help-seeker to go away and find another way out.

Legend has it that Su Laosan completely disappeared from the teahouse stage when it was fashionable to post such slogans as "do not talk about national affairs" in teahouses.

The courtyard of the Zen Tea room in Today's Daci Temple, quiet and elegant, but with less literati and market atmosphere.

"Agritainment" like this is distributed in large and small community gardens in Chengdu.

The open-air tea garden of Caotang Temple. Chengdu culturati often bring guests from other places to drink tea here.

This is also a "tea drinking day." Only for that it has turned cloudy, so it's time for tea drinkers to go home.

Daci Temple after restoration into a temple.

Daci Temple located in the downtown area. The temple in the Tang Dynasty (AD 618–907) was a place for literati to drink tea and chat after the Republic of China. In 2004, it was restored into a temple.

2

Memory

How many great men were forgotten through the ages?
Great drinkers are better known than sober sages.

—Li Bai

There is nothing that people fear more than the loss of memory. A person who has lost his memory is not much different from the walking dead. What about a city? If it loses its memory, is it not the same as being dead? My friend said indignantly, "Chengdu is a city without memory." This friend loves architecture, and he talked about urban memory from the perspective of architecture. He said that the new houses and streets everywhere deprive the city of its past, and without a past, is there a future? Maybe it is too radical to define Chengdu in this way, but I understand his feelings. I've heard that the buildings and streets in many European cities have their own "memory," such as Paris and Prague. Not long ago, I heard a story about Deng Xiaoping, a man from Sichuan who studied in France in his early years and often bought a kind of snack from a cafe on a corner of the street in Paris. Decades later, Deng Xiaoping, a Chinese leader, revisited Paris and felt nostalgic, so he asked his staff to buy the snack in the cafe. To his surprise, the staff successfully bought it. However, my friend said if you stayed at home for one month in Chengdu, you would get lost in the streets. It may be exaggerated a little, but almost exactly in terms of the speed of transformation of Chengdu's old city over the years.

Teahouses on Qintai Road.

But I still don't think Chengdu is a city without memory.

It is not always the material things that can evoke our memories. A building, a monument, a book, a painting, a photograph, a clay pot, or even a tree or a river bay are the most "real" things that remind us of the past. Still, something else that seems less "real," i.e., something non-material there tenaciously perpetuating our memories—for example, folklore, an art form or a traditional craft. Among the cultural heritage of humanity recognized by UNESCO, there are intangible cultural heritage and tangible cultural heritage. The Chinese Dragon Boat Festival, Nuo Opera, Xinjiang Uyghur Mukam (a folk song and dance), Xi'an Drum Music, and Yixing Zisha-making are not yet recognized by the relevant UN agencies,* but their forms fit very well the definition of "intangible cultural heritage of humanity" (i.e., oral transmission and language as a cultural carrier; traditional performing arts, including opera, music, dance, music, acrobatics, etc.; folklore activities, rituals, festivals; traditional folk knowledge and practices about nature and the universe; traditional handicraft skills; cultural space related to the above expressions) already. It reminds me of the Chengdu teahouse and the way of life of the Chengdu people in the teahouse. Is it somehow related to the "intangible cultural heritage of humanity"?

Don't get me wrong. I don't mean to encourage the people of Chengdu to "apply for the list of cultural heritage" with the "folklore" of having fun in the teahouses (I'd be crazy to do that). I'm just trying to illustrate that, as far as the buildings and streets are concerned, even if Chengdu becomes a new city

---

*When the author wrote this article, only Kunqu Opera (2001) and Guqin Art (2003) were included in the "Representative List of Intangible Cultural Heritage of Humanity" in China.

without a so-called "past," the memories of the city will still be tenaciously passed on in other forms. And the teahouse is undoubtedly one such form.

My memory of Chengdu teahouses started in 1983 when I visited Chengdu for the first time. Having no friends there, I, as a tourist, mainly drank tea in those teahouses in the parks. From 1986 onwards, I had more friends in Chengdu, and the places I drank tea also began to "deepen," so I got to know those teahouses hidden in the streets and alleys. At that time, my friends generally did not have telephones at home, let alone beepers. If we wanted to meet, we must go to his house directly. The Chengdu friends I knew were all poets. I once said lyrically that it was through poetry that I developed a friendship and relationship with the city. Among these poets, the closest ones were Lan Ma, Yang Li, and Shang Zhongmin, and of course, Lan Ma's wife at that time, Liu Tao, and Yang Li's wife at that time, Xiao An, who were also excellent poets. We were a school of poetry, called "Fei Fei." At that time, Lan Ma lived in Zhuanlun Street in Yanshikou, Shang Zhongmin lived in Song Xianqiao in the Hydropower School, and Yang Li lived in XinEr Village. I remember that we often rode bicycles to XinEr Village, standing on the street and calling on Yang Li to go downstairs. Then went to a nearby teahouse and stayed for half a day.

The teahouses in XinEr Village were the most common teahouse in Chengdu, like the kinds that spread in various neighborhoods and small streets in Chengdu. In a room beside the street, there were 6 to 9 square tables with four bamboo chairs for each, which thus formed a teahouse. There was "three flowers" tea at the price of 1 yuan per bowl, and the most expensive "Mao Feng" at 3 yuan per bowl. Yang Li said that in earlier times, you could drink a bowl of "three flowers" for just 30 fens. The bowl used to make tea was made of earthenware, a little bit rough.

A copper pot was also generally used to pour tea, but the teahouse attendants were casual and not as fancy and elaborate as the legend said when pouring tea. Yang Li often played chess with his high school classmates in the teahouse. One of them was called Wang Jing, who had the highest level of weiqi among them. He was the administrator of the library of Sichuan University, but as far as I remember, he hardly ever worked. I heard Yang Li say that there was a time when Wang Jing took sick leave and spent all day in the teahouse playing weiqi, but he did not seem to have trained to the point

It looks like a window from a distance, but it is a teahouse when you approach it.

The open-air tea garden at the head of the old Nanmen Bridge (formerly Wanli Bridge). When I lived on Hongmen Street in 1992, I often drank tea with people here. With a bowl of "three flowers," we could drink from noon to dusk.

of being able to play weiqi for a living. Yang Li said it was not that Wang Jing was not as skilled as others, but he was too honest to disguise himself. One could not make a living by playing gambling weiqi in the teahouse if he was too honest to disguise even if he was a master in weiqi, because people who knew you played well, simply did not play with you. You would be alone and have no opportunity to show your "martial arts." So, generally, people who played weiqi for a living had to hide their real level skillfully and leave some false impressions on people. There was once a master, but I forgot his name. According to Yang Li, he was at least No. 2 or 3 dan grading. Every time he played, no matter how weak the other player was, he always beat the rival a little, making people feel that he won every game narrowly, a fluke. The loser also thought that he was not much worse, or even not worse than the other side. As long as he concentrated more, a little more carefully, he would certainly win if there was one more game. So, people would go to the teahouse to play a game or one more game with the hidden master every day. Of course, these people would almost always lose. The loss was not too much, but only a little. In this way, this master would not lack an opportunity to win money. What was more interesting was that this master had a habitual action when playing weiqi; that is, he tended to shake his head and sigh unconsciously after a move, as if regretting that he had made a wrong move. This habitual action has fooled many innocent people.

However, there was once a time, I couldn't remember which year it was, but I heard from Yang Li that it was in the 1980s when a Japanese amateur weiqi delegation came to Chengdu and beat all the players in Chengdu. These old Japanese men and women defeated even the professional players in Chengdu then. Under the doubts of "there was nobody that can win in Shu?" he couldn't stand it any longer, and this unknown master in the teahouse came forward with surprising performance, became famous overnight, and won glory for the people of Chengdu and even for the Chinese people. However, after being a hero, his livelihood was a problem. Think about it, when he walked into the teahouse, who else dared to play with him? Luckily, there was an entrepreneur in Chengdu, Mr. Gong, the general manager of Chengdu Cigarette Factory, who was an enthusiast of weiqi. When he heard about the situation, he recruited him into his factory as a union cadre. And this was once a good story among weiqi fans.

In the 1980s, singing Sichuan opera and storytelling seemed no longer popular in teahouses in Chengdu, but projecting videos became popular. That was the era when Hong Kong martial arts films were popular. Yang Li said that one year, he had a business to do with a friend. It was a ready-made business, and as long as you were willing to run errands, the money could be in hand. However, it was the time when the teahouse projected *The Legend of the Condor Heroes*. He and this friend spent five yuan a day immersing themselves in the teahouse to watch the video. By the time they finished dozens of episodes of *The Legend of the Condor Heroes* and dizzied out of the teahouse, the business in hand went down the drain.

In the summer of 1992, I officially settled in Chengdu. We, Yang Li, Lan Ma, Ji Mu Langge, Shang Zhongmin, some former "Fei Fei" poets, and I, set up an advertising agency together. We also often sat in teahouses. But at that time, we didn't talk about poetry but advertising. In that year, Chengdu was full of companies. Our company had workplaces, while many more companies didn't have any. The so-called "company," in fact, was a state of its owner walking around with a briefcase or a teahouse he was sitting in causally. Talking about business had always been a tradition in Chengdu teahouses. Therefore, even if we had a fixed office location with one or two office rooms where we wrote a big slogan like "Opening the Second Chapter of China's Advertising Industry" and equipped with a 386 computer to match the slogan, we still preferred to meet with clients in a teahouse. In addition to living habits, I think it might be easier for teahouses to give people the feeling of "equality." Because no matter whether you were Party A or Party B, when each person put a bowl of tea on the table, no one can be condescending when talking. Of course, in the conversation, Party A is obviously more confident. However, because of this, Party B's tone will also become larger. Because this was a teahouse, everyone could brag.

It's also the same to this day. Chengdu people like to talk business, talk about things, and socialize in teahouses. For example, if you were the boss of a company, you had your employees and an office room, faxes, computers, etc., and there is no shortage of office equipment. But you don't like sitting upright like a boss in the executive chair behind a big writing desk. You drive to the company at 10 or 11 every morning, issue a few documents, ask your subordinates to come in and explain a few things, and then go to the teahouse you often go to. There, you can read newspapers and communicate with your subordinates or customers on the phone. At noon, you can order a bowl of spare ribs or braised beef noodles. After lunch, you can lie on the large and comfortable rattan sofa and nap. During the whole afternoon, you can either make an appointment with clients to talk about things that are difficult to talk about in the office in a relaxed and casual environment; and modern office facilities such as telefax and surfing the internet are generally available in the better teahouses. When there is no business to talk about, you can invite several friends to play cards together, make a small bet, let one of them win the dinner money today, and then have a meal together.

From 1994 to 1996, there was a teahouse called "Ming Qing Teahouse" on Kehua North Road. At that time, I was working in a nightclub above this teahouse. My friends who used to write poetry, such as Li Yawei and Ma Song, suddenly transformed from "reckless poets" into "booksellers." But their "reckless" habits were still there, fond of living in no fixed place and settling down anywhere all over the world. As soon as they returned to Chengdu, they were bound to gather in the Ming Qing Teahouse, directly making it their sitting room, living room, editorial department, chess home, love hut, and food group. Some of the best-selling books were planned and

Located on the left side of the former People's Committee Guest House (now the National Hotel), Min Taste Teahouse is one of the earliest teahouses in Chengdu. This nostalgic spot holds cherished memories for many people.

The round arch at the entrance of Zhen Liu Tea Garden.

programmed out in this teahouse. After the nightclub's closure in 1996, in my first full-length novel, which I wrote after going back home—*Pan Jinlian Memoirs*, there were chapters in which this teahouse was set as the backdrop for the story. And I also had a short story, the title of which was simply "Ming Qing Teahouse."

There was also a teahouse called "South Wind" on Hongxing Road, next to the Sichuan Daily Newspaper. This area gathered most of the media in Chengdu, and thus was a place where journalists gathered. South Wind teahouse once became reporters' "private teahouse," where writing, relaxing, bragging, and exchanging information could take place. Sometimes, some lazy journalists did not even go to the news scene but just ran to the "South Wind" and could get the "news release" from the journalists who went to the scene. Therefore, some people also jokingly called the "South Wind" "the second news site." When I read Deng Muqing's *Old Lores in Chengdu* (Chengdu Times Publishing House, April 2005 edition), I found that history had a surprising repetition that the old Chengdu news reporters also often made the teahouse a "second work area." "In General House Street on the corner of Chunxi North Road, there was a famous teahouse called 'Zhuo River,' where newspaper apprentices (journalists) must gather every day at noon. They exchanged news and created public opinion there, and they snatched a little leisure from a busy life." (*Old Lores in Chengdu*) The book also wrote that sometimes the associate editor asked the writer to write a manuscript in the teahouse. It was also highly similar to today. When the *Business Morning Post* had to start a new supplement in 2000, the editor asked a group of writers to go to the Daci Temple for tea to determine what column each of us would write. Later, there have been many such cases. Isn't this kind of "talking about things" in the teahouse also "folklore"?

South Wind Teahouse probably should be considered the earliest "high-end" teahouse in Chengdu after the reform and opening up. It was about 1993 when Yang Li and I were still running a company engaged in advertising. A few Chengdu businessmen who came back from Hainan came to us and said they wanted to open a teahouse in Chengdu and asked us to make an advertising program and design some printed materials with the corporate VI logo. We were unsure if Chengdu people, deeply rooted in the simplicity and casualness of the teahouse, would accept this kind of high-end foreign teahouse. Despite the doubts, we still took this business. As it turned out, the Chengdu market seemed ready for such a teahouse. The first one opened and became popular immediately, followed by the second and third. Chengdu is a city that accepts pop culture quickly, not only good at accepting it, but also good at transforming it. At first, the Chengdu teahouse clearly carried traces of imitation of the coastal teahouse, with a little western and a little Cantonese flavor, which was "Copinism." Later, there were more Chinese-style teahouses that obviously carried the characteristics of western Sichuan dwellings (the decoration style of Ming Qing Teahouse mentioned above was an example).

And then to the appearance of "Sentosa" outside Yangxi Line 2nd Ring Road, Chengdu had the so-called "most high-end" teahouse. Many years had passed, and I did not know if it was still considered the leader in the teahouse industry. For many years after it opened, I only heard of its name but never had the opportunity to visit it, because I knew it was so expensive that my income could not afford it. I could not understand what made it so expensive until 2001, when one of my friends in Nanjing, Han Dong, came to Chengdu. An old friend of his, who returned to Chengdu from the United States to visit relatives, invited him to "Sentosa," and I was also invited to keep them company. I then saw the true face of this leader in the Chengdu teahouse industry.

I was a little late that day, and they had arrived first. I took a taxi from the south gate, and when I arrived at the entrance of "Sentosa," a tall, dignified, and attentive porter opened the door for me. When I entered the lobby, an attendant took a look at me and greeted me in a warm and friendly way: "Is this Mr. He? Please go up to the third floor." Then, she led me into the elevator. As soon as I got out of the elevator on the third floor, another attendant also enthusiastic and friendly, was already waiting at the entrance: "Is this Mr. He? Mr. Han is waiting for you in room 303." Then, she

Street performers performing juggling in the tea garden by the river. In the 1990s, in the tea garden by the river on Binjiang Road, a thin old man was often seen, dressed in red, performing this juggling of bottles, but I have not seen him in recent years.

Drinking tea, basking in the sun, cleaning ears ... The life of the Chengdu people is misunderstood as "rotten" by the outside world, and it seems that it is not completely accidental.

guided me to the corridor to the private room. After being served like this, I understood why "Sentosa" was so expensive. Such service is not unique but rare in Chengdu's teahouses.

Chengdu's teahouses were also changing, but no matter how they changed, luxurious or foreign (referring to the foreign style of the teahouse decoration and facilities), the mentality of tea drinkers remained the same. Let's just say that the chairs in the common teahouses now are not the traditional bamboo chairs that are iconic for Chengdu teahouses, most of which are sofa-style rattan chairs. I think the rattan chair is similar to the bamboo chair; that is, it is very comfortable for people to sit in it. If the chairs are uncomfortable, no matter what kind of teahouse you want to run, you will not run it successfully, because Chengdu people want to "live" in teahouses, not just to drink tea. Like a western chair in a coffee shop, if it is not for the "powder" (beautiful lady) to have an "appointment," it is difficult for a man to sit for half an hour. The humanistic tradition of a leisure city like Chengdu has been created because of this pursuit of comfort. This tradition is reflected in the teahouse; that is, the family atmosphere of the teahouse remains unchanged, and the lifestyle of Chengdu people in the teahouse remains unchanged too. You may have been away from Chengdu for a long time, and when you come back, you may don't know the road, and the streets and houses are very unfamiliar to you, but as soon as you enter the teahouse, you will feel: I am back in Chengdu again. Or, an outlander who has only read books such

The "three-piece" of lidded-bowl tea.

as *Old Lores in Chengdu, Old Chengdu during the Republic of China*, and *Chengdu: Hibiscus Autumn Dream* but has never been to Chengdu, will naturally get that sense of identity as long as he walks into a teahouse and stays for a long time, well, this is indeed the legendary Chengdu.

3

Lidded-Bowl Tea and the Others

Without a teahouse, there would be no life.

—Sha Ting

Lidded-Bowl Tea

When people talk about teahouses, one of the first words to be used is "Lidded-Bowl Tea." Whenever you talk about drinking Lidded-Bowl Tea, it is inevitable that you are talking about Chengdu teahouses.

Lidded-Bowl Tea is named after the tea set. The tea set is also known as a "three-piece," which is a combination of three pieces, a tea bowl, a bowl lid, and a tea saucer. Lidded-Bowl Tea is unique to Chengdu teahouses. Its tea bowl, bowl lid, and tea saucer all have a symbolic meaning: "the sky covers it (bowl lid), the earth carries it (tea saucer), and people nurture it (tea bowl)." And the unique feature of the Lidded-Bowl Tea lies in the tea saucer, also known as the "tea boat," which is a plate to bear the tea bowl and was invented in Chengdu by the daughter of Cui Ning, Governor of the western part of Sichuan Province in Jianzhong years (780–783) of Emperor Dezong of Tang Dynasty according to the legend. The original teacup did not have an underlay and often scalded fingers, so Cui Ning's daughter invented a wooden plate to support the teacup. In order to prevent the cup from tipping over easily when drinking tea, she also tried to use wax to wrap the center of the wooden tray so that the cup could be easily fixed. This was the earliest tea saucer. Today's tea saucers are made of ceramics, the same material as tea bowls; they are also made of metal (white iron). The beauty of drinking Lidded-Bowl Tea is that there is a lid on the tea bowl, which can keep the tea in a warm state and plays the function of steaming the tea leaves and enhancing the flavor of the tea; removing the lid can also dissipate heat, and one can adjust at will that the tea can be warmer or cooler; when holding up the tea bowl with the tea saucer and tilt it obliquely or halfway toward the mouth, you can slowly sip the tea from the gap between the tea bowl and the lid. As a result, not only can the tea leaves in the tea be prevented from being poured into the mouth, but also the drinking posture is very elegant and stylish.

Bamboo Chairs

If it is said that Lidded-Bowl Tea is the characteristic symbol of the Chengdu teahouse, then I would say that the bamboo chair is the "secret weapon" of the Chengdu teahouse.

Anyone who has run a teahouse knows that to be successful in business, it must be popular; an effective way is that the chairs of the teahouse must be able to retain people. In the past, I have sat in a riverside teahouse in Chongqing, with high square tables and long benches, but no matter what kind of body position I adopted, I couldn't sit still for the time taken to smoke a cigarette, and I felt a sore back and wanted to leave. However, the bamboo chairs in Chengdu are different. There are backrests and armrests. The height and hardness of the backrest, and the width and angle of the armrests are all in line with the structure of the human body, and thus it is very comfortable to sit on. In addition, the tea table is generally only knee-high, which is very convenient

Vacant bamboo chairs.

for drinking, so I believe that the biggest "commercial secret" of Chengdu teahouses which can last for hundreds of years is this bamboo chair. I remember watching a program on Chengdu TV last year, which introduced a French lady who was probably funded by a French institution and came to Chengdu to study teahouse culture. When the host asked her: "If you were asked to bring an item from Chengdu back as a souvenir, what would you most like to bring?" She replied that it must be a bamboo chair.

Urn

In the past, the stove for boiling water in the old teahouse in Chengdu was not called a "stove" but an "urn," which was about two meters long and one meter wide, with upper and lower levels. The higher level was a real urn, storing hot water. In winter, tea guests could buy hot water in the urn to warm their feet if they felt cold with their feet after sitting for a long time. The teahouse was equipped with foot basins, and a basin of foot-washing water was equivalent to the fee for a bowl of tea. The lower one was the clay hearth for boiling water, the surface of which was covered with steel plates, and the steel plates were cut with round holes. The size of the holes was the same as that of the bottom of the pot. The flame jumped out of the hole and burned the bottom of the pot directly. Sometimes the attendant came to fetch water before it was boiled, and the "Master" (the person who boiled the water) would lift the teapot and use the "fire drill" to poke the fire. The flames jumped high with the spark, making the pot of water boil in an instant.

The boiled water in the urn was not only used for making tea in teahouses, but also provided boiled and hot water for daily drinking for people in the neighborhood. Going in and out of the teahouse with the tea bottle (thermos flask) or washbasin was a part of the daily life of Chengdu people in the past, just like queuing up to go to the public toilet and emptying the toilet in the early morning. Therefore, in the past, a rental house would be specially marked in a rental notice: there is a teahouse near the house. This showed that you didn't have to worry about boiling water and hot water after living here. What's more, when some people stewed a chicken or decocted medicinal herbs, they also took it to the urn of the teahouse. Of course, just as you had to pay for boiling water and hot water, you had to pay a little "fire fee" (that is, processing fee) for stewing chicken and decoction. These fees were generally collected by the master who took charge of the urn, and the owner of the teahouse would not get involved in it.

Maintaining Tea Leaves

The old teahouse in Chengdu was very particular about brewing tea. The water for brewing tea must be boiling water that had just been boiled. Pouring the first water (also known as "head water") to fill half a bowl, that was just covering the tea leaves. It's called "maintaining tea leaves." Wait until the tea leaves in the tea bowl change from dry to wet and stretch out before pouring the second water. At this time, hot boiling water was poured out from the long-mouthed big teapot with a hot mist, beating the tea leaves that had been stretched up and down in the tea bowl, like a dance, with the last sinking to the bottom of the bowl. A bowl of green and fragrant tea was presented in front of you. Even if you didn't drink it, it also pleased the eyes.

LEFT A teahouse worker carrying bamboo chairs. (The picture was provided by Jiang Hai, a friend of mine.)

ABOVE A copper teapot in old teahouses.

Dr. Tea

There is a general saying that Chengdu people don't care about the tea when they drink tea in the teahouse, but about the words. That is, drinking tea is not the purpose, but a place suitable for chatting is crucial. Therefore, unlike the southern "Kung Fu Tea," in which "tea ceremony" and "tea art" are paid special attention, its casual and civilian nature is also one of the reasons why Chengdu teahouses are so prosperous. However, if you think that Chengdu teahouses have no "kung fu" and "unique skills" at all, it would be a misunderstanding—it seems that Chengdu teahouses have been running for hundreds of years in vain.

Let's say pouring tea. "Seven or eight tea guests sitting around the low tea table and shouting 'tea please,' so the master would respond to it. You could see the master carrying the purple copper long-spout kettle with his right hand, five fingers of the left hand spreading apart, with a stack of tea bowls, tea lids, and tea saucers under his arm, came to the table and stretched his hands, then the tea saucers clanked on the table like flowers blossoming, stopping right in front of the guests respectively, which could be said to be all at their posts; then the master put the tea bowl loaded with tea on every tea saucer, and clasped the tea lid to be close to the tea bowl with his left hand. The purple copper long-spout kettle on his right hand was like a red dragon spitting water, pouring water to fill the bowl. When the bowl was almost full, the master held the kettle suddenly, followed by a flapping sound, turned the tea lid over, and covered the bowl. All the action was fast, clean, sharp, and really skillful" (quoted from Sichuan Online in "Sichuan Tea Art Has Formed into a Style")!

The master pouring tea was called an "attendant," also known as "Dr. Tea." In the past, the attendants in the teahouses not only kept their hands and feet busy, but also kept their mouths busy. They shared the news, rumors, and jokes with guests, and it seemed that they knew everything in the world, so they had a nickname of "Doctor"— in today's words, a complete "Ba Ye." Even so, Dr. Tea's reputation was not in the mouth but in hands and feet. In the 1950s, there was an old man named Fang Zhongyu, who was a well-known tea doctor in an old teahouse in Chengdu. He was once introduced in a film called *One of the Best in China*. The old man Fang Zhongyu was very skilled. He could stack up 15 sets of lidded bowls and pour water with both hands at the same time. "When the tea was finished, and guests saw off, he could hold a tea bowl in one hand, clasping the lid of the bowl with his thumb, and pour the remaining tea water without leaving any leaves, which could be rated as a unique skill." (quoted from Sichuan Online in "Sichuan Tea Art Has Formed into a Style").

There are not many tea doctors like this in today's teahouses. However, the art of pouring tea has not been lost. There are two brothers surnamed Liao in Chengdu Shunxing Old Teahouse, and their performances are eye-opening. In a national tea art competition, brothers Liao Dasong and Liao Xiaosong joined hands to perform a set of tea art with a double long-spout kettle. This set of tea art movements has a total change of 18 moves, such as: placing the hot copper kettle on the top of the head, and the slender water pouring down from the top, so this is called "boy worshiping Buddha"; bearing the copper kettle on the back with the kettle mouth attached to the back, the head bending down, leaning forward together with the kettle, and the water passes over the back and goes into the tea bowl, so this is called "bearing the thorns and pleads for sin"; then turning back and lowering the waist with face upward, placing the copper kettle on the chest, the long-sprout crosses over the throat, neck, and chin, and the pouring water passes over the face and goes into the tea bowl, so this is called "fishing the moon from the sea." After the full set of moves, one may feel dazzled. As a result, pouring tea has become not only a technique, but also an art. Dr. Tea can also be called an "artist."

Water in Sand Filters

In the past, there were patios in teahouses, and there were one or two large stone jars in the patios. The stone jars were also called "sand filters" because they were covered with pebbles, palm leaves, and fine sand from the suburban river. The "running water" (river water) transported from the river was poured into a sand filter, and after clarification, it was filtered by fine sand, palm leaves, and pebbles before being boiled on the urn for tea drinkers. The water in the sand filters was sweet and mellower than the well water. The tea brewed with it had a unique flavor. In the past, teahouses in Chengdu, especially the more powerful ones, all liked to stick out a "fragrant tea brewed with river water" flag in front of the door to attract customers. The reason was that the groundwater in Chengdu had a bitter taste, and it was not good to make tea with well water. Of course, there were exceptions. For example, the Xue Tao Well in Wangjianglou Park was said to have been a favorite place for teahouses to draw water in the past, and its water quality was better than "running water." It was so good that the teahouses in Chongqing all liked to come there to fetch the water, and showed that their tea was brewed by "water from Xue Tao Well."

Cigarette Sellers and Smokers in the Old Teahouse

In the old Chengdu teahouses, there were generally three types of cigarettes in the wooden box hanging around the neck of the cigarette sellers, namely paper cigarettes, leaf cigarettes, and a hookah. Paper cigarettes and leaf cigarettes were mostly sold by poor children. Most of these children had a wooden box in a shape of a dustpan hanging on their chests, which contained various brands of cigarettes. "Hartmann," "Old Knife," "Red Gold," and "Platinum Dragon" were popular among tea drinkers, while leaf cigarettes from Shifang and Jintang in Sichuan were the most popular among the elderly tea drinkers. The boy held a long bamboo cigarette stick in his hand and shouted along the tea table: "Paper cigarettes? Leaf cigarettes? Do you want one?" Most paper cigarettes could be sold separately, and the total price was slightly higher than the whole pack. The high part was the profit from selling cigarettes. Leaf cigarettes were for smokers to play with. When you wanted to smoke, you only needed to wave your hand, and a long cigarette rod with a polished copper cigarette holder would be handed to your mouth.

This pot is more like a teapot. It comes from the Song Dynasty (AD 960–1279).

Just raise your hand and open your mouth, and the cigarette seller would offer the cigarette and light it on your behalf, and the smoker would not bother at all. Of course, this service was more expensive. And what's the point of spending a little more money for people who want to play in style?

As for selling the hookah, the procedures were particularly detailed and complicated. First of all, the outfit for selling the hookah was unique: a large leather shoulder bag hanging bulgingly around the waist, and the bag was divided into several small compartments, each containing different varieties of hookah such as yellow silk and cotton cigarettes, and a bunch of paper was inserted outside. When the hookah smoker was about to smoke, the hookah seller was also on call, holding the huge special pipe (this was not the kind of copper hookah that every family had, but something similar to the western musical instrument "Saxophone"), handed a retractable cigarette holder to the smoker's mouth from afar, and then filled the cigarette and lit it on behalf of the smoker. The smoker did not need to move his hands or his head. While smoking, he could chat with other tea drinkers, and the craving for tobacco was satisfied after one pipe and another.

Jargon in Old Chengdu Teahouses

In the past, there were many conventional, unique, and interesting industry languages in Chengdu teahouses. For example: adding tea leaves was called "making leaves"; putting tea leaves into a tea bowl was called "grasping"; much tea in each bowl was called "full," and less tea was called "stingy"; originally drinking tea was called "eating tea"; pouring the boiled water into a tea bowl with tea leaves for the first time was called "soaking leaves" or "brewing tea"; if the temperature of the boiling water was not enough and the tea leaves could not sink to the bottom with some of them floating on the surface, this was called "it was not soaked well," which was ironically called "floating boat leaves"; after the boiling water had been placed for a long time and the temperature has dropped, this was called "tired," or "the water is tired"; when pouring boiling water into the tea bowl for the second time, this was called "adding" or "rushing"; drinking boiled water only without tea leaves was called "free with tea" or "glass"; when there were few customers, it was called "Diaotang"; when there were many customers, it was called "Dayongtang"; a cleaning rag was called "Suishou" or "exploring the water" at an earlier time ... "One lid" and "two lids" were commonly used words in teahouses. The "lid" here meant that the tea lid must be lifted every time the water was poured.

"White" meant after pouring boiling water many times, the tea had been soaked too long that there was no color, and it had become white water. "Guan" was in terms of matching the tea. Teahouses often match different grades and prices of tea leaves in a certain proportion, which was called "guan," also called "gou." The method of "guan" and "gou" were confidential.

The "three-piece" of lidded-bowl tea.

"Calling for the tea money" was a greeting for tea drinkers paying for the tea money for their friends. When you entered the teahouse, the acquaintance who arrived first would shout, "I will pay the tea money here for you," which was called "calling for the tea money." The more people call for tea money for you, the greater your face is, which shows that you have many friends and enjoy popularity and prestige.

"Replaced" meant to replace another new bowl of tea. When others were "calling for tea money," the person who was called for would bow his hands and say "replaced, replaced"; if there were many people calling, he had to say "replace altogether," which meant "together" or "completely." These were all fake hospitality, and there were very few "replaced" ones indeed.

"Uncover the lid" meant to drink tea symbolically. When someone paid tea money for you and tea was brewed, even if you felt too full to drink it, or you were too busy to drink it, you had to lift the tea lid and swing it in the tea bowl to take a symbolic sip; otherwise, it was impolite.

Chengdu Old Teahouse with the Nature of the Gang

In the late Qing Dynasty and the Republic of China, some of the teahouses in Chengdu were gathering places for Pao Ge organizations or business gangs. For example, Anle Temple Teahouse was for the grain and oil industry; Xianju Teahouse on Xiadong Street was for the gauze industry; "Liufang" on Shangdong Street, "Juchunlou" on Chengshou East Street, and Qinghe Teahouse on the Chunxi South Road were for the silk industry; Xinshangchang Teahouse on the opposite of Anle Temple, Jianglou Teahouse on Chunxi East Road, and "Guanlan Pavilion" in Dakejia Lane were for the printing industry; Weijiaci Teahouse on Admiral Street was for the leather shoe industry; Pinxiang Teahouse was the trading market for guns and opium; the teahouse at the entrance of Duyuan Street was the gathering place for martial artists in the whole city; a few other teahouses were the meeting places for the fellow townsmen's associations and classmates' associations. There were dozens of association signs hanging in the teahouses of Zhongshan Park (today's Cultural Palace), such as the Fushun County Travel Province Hometown Association and the Pingshan County Travel Province Students Association.

Other Old Chengdu Teahouses

Other famous teahouses in old Chengdu that I found only in Deng Muqing's *Old Lores in Chengdu* and Mr. Liushahe's *Chengdu: Hibiscus Autumn Dream* are "Visit Tao Village" at the head of Jiuyan Bridge, which is presumably named for its proximity to the former residence Wangjianglou of the Tang Dynasty poetess Xue Tao; "Deep in the Forest" in the bamboo grove on Jinhua Street in Beimen; "Yuhe Island" at the head of Wanfu Bridge; "Geshuo Pavilion" on Hua Pai Fang Street outside the old Ximen; "the Summer Palace," "Shuquan Lou," "Yin Tao," and "Yi Zhi" on Chunxi Road; the Chunxi Teahouse behind the bronze statue of Sun Yat-sen; the "Zhuo River" on General Mansion Street was a place where newsmen used to gather; the Huahua Teahouse on East Street, the largest teahouse in Chengdu at that time, could seat thousands of people drinking tea in the same room and was a place where businessmen frequently visited; the "Lu Yu House" on Yudaiqiao Street, named after "tea sage" Lu Yu (Tang Dynasty, author of the world's first tea monograph *Tea Classic*), was the "sitting" place for the performance of the famous Yangqin artist Li Decai (De Wa Zi); "Jin Chun House" on Chengen East Street was the "sitting" place for the performance of the famous anklong artist "Blind Jia" (Shu San). With a bamboo tube and two pieces of bamboo instruments, he could sing the momentum of a thousand troops, so some scholars and writers wrote an article "Three Greats in Chengdu Jinchun Lou" and published in the newspaper based on Blind Jia's singing on Jinchun Lou, Zhou Mazi's skills of pouring tea for the tea customers, and Fatty Si's peanuts sold upstairs; there was also the Ju Xian Teahouse at the north entrance of the main street of the Zitong Bridge, the "Ou Xiang Pavilion" on Wenmiao Street, the "Linjiang Pavilion" on Fencaohu Street, the "Guangchun Pavilion" in Shanxi Pavilion, "Xiangquanju" in Beidajin Street, "Furongting" in Gulou North Street, "Jiangshang Village" outside the New South Gate, "Yinxiao"

The shape of teapots and bowls in the Ming and Qing dynasties is not much different from today.

The murals unearthed from the Han tomb present the scene of brewing tea in ancient times.

in Huangchengba (around the present Provincial Exhibition Hall), "Liang Yuan" in Changshun Street, and "Xiao Yuan" in Shuncheng Street, etc.; and still "Yuelai Tea Garden" in Huaxing Street, which still exists today, was the "theater nest" of the Sichuan opera troupe "Sanqinghui."

It can be seen from the above that almost all urban streets in Chengdu had teahouses. The so-called proverb—"Half of a city's dwellers are tea drinkers," was not a lie.

Why are there so many teahouses in Chengdu?

People have made the following analysis and summary of many of the teahouses in Chengdu from ancient times to the present:

- The Chengdu Plain produces a lot of tea, but it's difficult to transport to other provinces. Therefore, the price of tea is very low, and there are many tea drinkers.
- The water in Chengdu is unclean and alkaline, and the water can only be drunk after boiling. Teahouses meet this need.

- In the past, transportation in the Chengdu Plain mainly relied on unicycles, trolleys, sliding poles, etc., and the teahouse was a good place for laborers to rest.
- There is lots of slack farming time. Since Li Bing repaired Dujiangyan, the farmland on the Chengdu Plain has almost been irrigated by the artesian flow. Farmers only need to fertilize and remove weeds after planting rice in the spring until the autumn harvest. There was more slack time, and the teahouse was a good place to chat.
- Sichuan people like to eat stimulating food (such as pepper, chili pepper, etc.), so drinking tea can reduce excessive stimulation.

In addition to the above five points, I would like to add three more:

- Chengdu people have a bit of a "Pao Ge" habit in that they are good at making friends and meddling. Teahouses are an indispensable place for this.
- Chengdu is an inland basin with heavy water vapor and little sunlight. People in such a climate will inevitably feel depressed. Therefore, Chengdu people like to "get together," and teahouses are naturally a good place to "get together."
- Chengdu people are born to be talkative, and they are "talkative buns." When talking in a teahouse, there is no danger of a dry mouth, and no shortage of enthusiastic listeners.

In addition, soaking in the teahouse has become a custom, which has the function of "education" passed down from generation to generation. had this remark in his autobiography: "There are many teahouses in Chengdu, and there are friendly conversations in them that last for three hours. My generation grew up under the influence of these customs, so we were fond of delicious food and chatting. It was still difficult to remove this habit when studying abroad." It's difficult to change the custom of drinking tea, so the number of teahouses has been prosperous.

Hibiscus is the city flower of Chengdu. Drinking tea under hibiscus flowers is poetic in the eyes of outsiders, but it is a common practice for Chengdu people.

The female tea drinker who sat on the Sanhualou and meditated . . .

4

To Search and Visit

The next morning, I got up early, went for a walk on the street, and sat in a teahouse. The teahouse looked like a melon shed in Beijing, with a roof and a few long tables and benches. Tea was charged two yuan per person. I sat down and listened to the old man at the table next to him chatting. I was half a Chongqing native, so I understood half of it. I just heard an old man saying that he went to Germany when he was young ... Another old woman pouted and patted her legs, laughing at him for bragging. The wrinkles on her face gathered together, but the corners of her eyes were innocent and coquettish. Since then, I fell in love with Chengdu, because one of my ideals is to brag with a few old acquaintances when I get old, to be coquettish and angry, and to drink tea and eat together.

—Yin Lichuan, "Spring in Chengdu"

October 7, 2005

Seeing the sun come out in the afternoon, I decided to take my camera out and start my search for teahouses in Chengdu.

In order to take some photos for this book, I went to Digital City and bought a Nikon COOLPIX P2 digital camera. While sitting on the No. 78 bus, my right hand was excitedly holding this camera. To be honest, I was still confident in my photography skills. I still had an "Oriental" 135 camera that I bought in 1979 at home. In addition, a photo printing amplifier, which was also purchased in 1979, was still sitting on the top of the bookcase, covered with dust. These two items, together with several thick black-and-white family albums, proved that I was not too much to call myself a "skilled" photographer in this business.

Today's destination was People's Park. When doing the deskwork, I learned that there were two old teahouses inside People's Park; one was "Heming," and another was "Zhen Liu." The late old man Deng Muqing said in his book *Old Lores in Chengdu*: "Crossing the Jinhe Bridge from Ancestral Hall Street, a few steps away, there is a teahouse called 'Zhen Liu,' and its signboard is still the autography of celebrities Xie Wuliang. It is the place where high school and middle school students will meet on Sundays. Drinking tea near it is also fun." This referred to the 1930s and 1940s. Today, since the Jinhe River was nowhere to be seen, there was naturally no bridge over the Jinhe River that we could cross. Fortunately, the teahouse called "Zhen Liu" was still there. But on the signboard, the characters of "Zhen Liu Tea Garden" are no longer the handwriting of the famous Xie Wuliang in the past, but the writing of today's top-level Wei Minglun. I don't know calligraphy well, but I think Mr. Wei's handwriting should be good. However, it's a pity that I didn't see Xie Wuliang's autography. Elder Deng Muqing once described Xie Wuliang in *Old Lores in Chengdu*, saying that he was a

The brook in People's Park.

prodigy who could have achieved good fame, but he despised the imperial examinations and disdained taking the test. Being an illiterate person, he then held the post of supervisor (principal) in Chengdu 'Cungu School' which contains 'cultivated talent' students." It also said that his calligraphy style was unique, which was called "children's style" by the world. "At first glance, it looked like hand-painted graffiti; at the second glance, there was some innocence in it … It had not only the robustness of the Han and Wei steles, but also the beauty of the Jin and Tang dynasties. Rigorous parts were like a formal script, and flowing parts were like grass style, graceful and dignified parts were like Yan style, thin and strong parts were like Liu style …" (*Old Lores in Chengdu*)

In this way, if the word "Zhen Liu" by talent Xie still existed, my generation could also have a glimpse of his style.

Entering through the round arch with the signboard of "Zhen Liu Tea Garden," one could see the inside was surrounded by bamboo and shaded by green trees. Several square tables and bamboo chairs were placed among the bamboo, wood, and flowers. Under the mottled light and shadow, I saw many tea guests, and the seats were full. Amid the roar of voices, there was the sound of crashing mahjong. This scene was quite different from what the word "Zhen Liu" indicated in the past.

"A few dozen steps further, it was the only remaining 'Heming' with a history of several decades in this park after liberation." (*Old Lores in Chengdu*) But according to my steps, from "Zhen Liu" to "Heming," it was far more than a few dozen steps. From this, I inferred that the new Zhen Liu Tea Garden was probably not built on the original site of the former "Zhen Liu." Moreover, when Deng Muqing wrote this article (in 1997), there probably was not the restored "Zhen Liu" that I see today.

If you want to tell the location of "Heming" simply, you should go in from the main entrance of People's Park, walk straight for a few steps, then turn left, and you will see the quaint gatehouse with the word "Heming" inscribed. When I was doing the deskwork, I was still imagining: what exactly does this "Heming" teahouse look like? At first sight, it turned out to be the place where I often met three or five friends for tea in the early years. It's just that I only talked about tea and chat before, but I didn't notice the two big characters with a certain origin on the gatehouse. "In those days, 'Heming' was also a recreational place for scholars and celebrities. Xie Wuliang, Meng Wentong, Liu Boliang, Han Wenqi, etc., were almost regular customers here. Across the river from 'Heming' was the 'Green Pavilion.' For the sake of business, it advertised that the water with which they brewed tea was transported from Xue Tao Well. There were many people who drank morning tea. There was a 'Yongju Teahouse' adjacent to the east of the 'Green Pavilion,' and most of the drinkers were the elderly. It also organized chess tournaments each autumn." (*Old Lores in Chengdu*) But after I took my camera and walked around the park, I didn't find the "Green Pavilion" and "Yongju Teahouse" mentioned

Shao City Garden.

in Deng Muqing's book, but walked into a garden within a garden with a signboard of "Shao City Garden."

By the way, People's Park used to be called "Shao City Park." I can't remember which dynasty it was. Anyway, it was in ancient times. Chengdu was divided into two parts: the Big City and the Shao City. The Big City was in the east, and the Shao City was in the west. Many people mistakenly thought that Shao City was built by the Manchus, but it was actually not. It's just that after the Manchus came to Chengdu, they circled the old Shao City as the main settlement of the banner people. Later, the life of the bannermen became difficult, and their leader, the Governor of the Qing court in charge of Sichuan, came up with a way to open up the courtyards of the bannermen and make them into parks for the citizens to visit, and the ticket revenue was used for Bannerman's subsidy. This was the origin of Shao City Park.

Today, the "Shao City Garden" I walked into seems to still retain some of the pattern and style of the private gardens of the bannermen in the past, including rockeries, cloisters, flower paths, and lotus ponds, as well as a three-story wooden building with Ming and Qing architectural style. In front of them, there were people taking pictures beside the rockery, playing chess, and chatting in the corridor. The open space around the lotus pond and in the three-story wooden building was full of people drinking tea.

When I looked up and took a picture of that wooden building, I suddenly had a thought, could this be the "Thick Shade Teahouse" mentioned in Deng Muqing's article?

"Across a stream to the north of 'Yongju,' there is also a teahouse called 'Thick Shade.' When Xie Dekan, Huang Muyan, etc. proposed to build the 'Chengdu Weiqi Club,' this building was used as the club's site, and the president was Liu Fuyi. At that time, Du Wenyuan, a member of the

Sichuan Provincial Government, known as 'Old Du,' and later Xiao Du (Du Junguo), who was successful in weiqi, and Jia Titao, a famous weiqi player, all liked to fight upstairs there. Chess was also played upstairs, often crowded." (*Old Lores in Chengdu*)

October 8, 2005

Today is another sunny day. I decided to go to a few places with my camera. As we all know, Chengdu has little sunshine. As soon as the sun comes out, the open-air tea gardens are very popular. At this time, basking in the sun has become the main reason to go out, and drinking tea is only because the place where you drink tea is good for basking in the sun. There are many open-air tea gardens in Chengdu where you can sit and bask in the sun, covering almost every corner of Chengdu. Now, if I want to make some introductions, I feel a little messy and unable to write about it. The People's Park that I went to yesterday, as well as such places as Wangjianglou Park, Wuhou Temple, Du Fu Thatched Cottage, and Yongling (Wang Jian's Tomb) are all good places to drink tea and bask in the sun. Some temples, such as Wenshu Monastery, Zhaojue Temple, and Qingyang Temple, also have open-air tea seats. Along the Jinjiang River, it is also the first choice for people to invite friends to drink tea and bask in the sun around Hejiang Pavilion and Rainbow Bridge. I can't find a seat if I arrive there late. Then there are lots of tea guests in some open spaces in front of some iconic public buildings, such as the Provincial Sports Center (Houzi Gate), the Provincial Museum (relocated to the new site of Huanhuaxi Scenic Spot in 2009 and renamed "Sichuan Museum"), the Provincial Gymnasium. Even on the roof of the "Wanli" building at the head of the old South Gate Bridge (the former Wanli Bridge), a strange ship-like building, there is an open-air tea garden. I suddenly remembered what many outsiders say about Chengdu. They said it was a "lazy" and "rotten" city because people here drank tea from Monday to Sunday and did nothing else. What's more, a foreign wine merchant from Shanghai once said to me half-jokingly and half-seriously that he suspected that all men in Chengdu "live off women rather than work for a living." This is, of course, a big misunderstanding. I think the main reason for this is probably that there are not only many teahouses in Chengdu, but also

The interior of Shao City Garden.

many open-air ones. Outsiders in a hurry can see such a prosperous tea-drinking scene that cannot be seen in their city, which causes the illusion. As far as I know, there are many places to have morning tea in Guangzhou, and people don't come out after a long time. But those places that sell morning tea are in hidden buildings and are not conspicuous, so they don't cause such a big "shock."

I don't want to go to so many open-air teahouses today, and I just plan to go to a few places where I usually go with my friends and take a few photos. The first one is the Provincial Museum, which has been mentioned many times in my novels. There is a small garden planted with bamboo, plantains and several other tall trees between the left side of the gate of the Provincial Museum and Renmin South Road. This is the place to drink "Yard Tea." The history of "Yard Tea"; in this place is at least ten years old. It seems that it was there when I first settled in Chengdu in 1992. I have a friend named Li Fan who is a frequent visitor there. Moreover, even if he does not invite friends, he often goes there for tea alone. He didn't seem to change places throughout the year, except for bad weather, because he didn't want to drink tea in bad weather. I once asked him why he was so fond of it. He had two reasons: first, the tea price here was fair at 5 yuan per bowl, and there was only tea of 5 yuan per bowl, no cheaper and no more expensive ones either. No matter what kind of friends come there, they would not distinguish between the high and low in the choice of tea. Being equal made them feel casual. Second, you could "wash your eyes." That was to say, according to his many years of experience, there were many "powders" (beautiful ladies) drinking tea here. Sitting here drinking tea was pleasing to the eyes and made you feel very much at ease. I especially agree with his second reason but disagreed with his feeling a little in that it's pleasing to the eyes, but not at ease, but flustered. At that time, the Provincial Museum was being demolished and had to be moved to the suburbs. I didn't know if the new commercial and residential buildings would affect this "Yard Tea."

The second place I got to was "Xiang Mu Lin." It is not far from the Provincial Museum, and it is also on the Renmin South Road, about one stop away, that is, in a street garden adjacent to the Sichuan University's West China Campus diagonally opposite the Provincial Education College. The feature here is that it is also open-air and can be covered by the sun. Still, it seems more convert than the Provincial Museum side because of its fenced-in garden pattern. My friend Ma Xiaobing and I have had tea here many times. Of course, drinking tea with Ma Xiaobing is not a shameful thing. We don't need to hide, but we just like the quiet place.

Going further north along Renmin South Road was the third filming location I went to today—"Avoidance" in the Jinjiang Hotel, which was written by the writer Jiechen many times in the column articles of *Book City* and *21st Century Business Report* and other media. Here I have to apologize to my "witch" friends because we once had an agreement not to make this place public. The reason for not making it public is that it is tranquil there, which is very suitable for their "witch gathering." Therefore, "Avoidance" is a secret name that the "witches" took privately, not the real name of this tea garden. The original name of this tea garden is "Wisteria Garden." Its characteristics are not only quietness because few people know about it, as mentioned above, but also that it is actually hidden in a tall and dense forest. Therefore, when it is too hot for other "Yard Teas" to keep people, you can also sit here for a long time with a cup of tea not only in spring and autumn, but also in the real summer. Many friends from other places have been brought to "Avoidance" by the "witches" to drink tea, and they all speak highly of it. At the same time, there is no exception to be told by the "witches" to keep it secret. The reason why I am making it public now is that my courage comes from my trust in the discovery ability of the "witches," and I believe they will never worry about finding a new "Avoidance." By the way, the minimum tea price here is 10 yuan. In such an "expensive' environment, the cost of 10 yuan per person is not high.

The street sign of the famous Broad Alley.

LEFT Open-air tea garden.

ABOVE The ancient rhyme of Shao City. The tea is a bosom friend.

There are still more than two hours before the sun sets. I want to go to Yongling, which is Wang Jian's tomb. It is located at Samdong Bridge. By bus No. 78, you can also go to two places: the Broad and Narrow Alley and Qintai Road.

The Broad Alley and the Narrow Alley are two old alleys that have been carefully preserved in the transformation of the old city of Chengdu in the past ten years. They were the places where the Manchu soldiers lived in the Qing Dynasty. The buildings are bungalows with gray walls and black tiles. There are only a few luxurious houses. The Broad Alley is not wide, and the Narrow Alley is even narrower. But in recent years, the Chengdu people, especially the Chengdu culturati, have cherished them very much. Owing to its name, many tourists come to visit them when arriving in Chengdu. Especially foreigners, who are used to seeing the bright high-rise buildings and wide roads, feel that although it is a bit narrow and dilapidated, drinking tea in this alley with a strong atmosphere of life, is really "close" to the ancient city of Chengdu. Therefore, it is not surprising that if an international youth hostel appears in Broad Alley, it will attract all kinds of backpackers from home and abroad to live here.

In Broad Alley, there are many places where you can drink tea along the street and in the courtyard. The "Old Song Teahouse" opened by Old Song is the most famous among them. Old Song looked to be in his 40s or 50s. He claimed to be a poet, and he posted many poetry lists written by himself on the doors and walls of the teahouse. Old Song's teahouse has a storefront, but the seats are basically placed along the street. There are trees along the street, and poems from Old Song are sometimes hung on the trees. Old Song became famous in 2004 when the government planned to re-plan the broad and narrow alleys and asked residents to relocate. The residents had their opinions on this and were reluctant to move. The news media also had some views, so this place once became the focus of attention. What's more, because some reporters had been drinking tea here all year round, and they especially liked to drink tea in Old Song's Teahouse, such things as interviewing, and taking pictures naturally happened more in Old Song's house. Old Song and his teahouse had been featured on TV and in newspapers many times, and

This teahouse poster is interesting.

The exterior view of Weiliu Teahouse.

more and more people knew about him. My friend Apan contributed a lot to this. Being a reporter for the *Chengdu Evening News* at the time, she had a special talk with Old Song before. I also drank tea at Old Song's store several times with friends from the media. We could drink tea until it was very late here because he had made several kinds of medicinal wine, and cooked a few side dishes. If we had drunk tea for a long time, we could also have dinner there.

However, since the summer of 2005, I heard that Broad and Narrow Alley were still surrounded by construction fences, and the demolition and renovation projects were started. I went to look today, and it is really a construction site. However, to my surprise, the Old Song Teahouse is still in business. On the street which was dug up in pieces, the small square tables and bamboo chairs are also placed, and there are several tea drinkers in the sun there. I smiled with my camera in my hand and said hello to Old Song. Old Song was smoking and took a look at the camera. We didn't say anything. Actually, I had prepared to meet an acquaintance here, but when I saw my friends Li Fang and his wife Meng Qiu, I was still a little surprised. Although we are in the same city, we haven't seen each other for several years. Li Fang is a painter who started to sell paintings for a living in recent years. Mengqiu is engaged in writing, and is also considered a freelance writer. Both of them do not work. I think they must also belong to the people who are looking for the "favorite" teahouse tea everywhere. Together with them, there is a "foreigner" called Li An. He is a famous Chengdu "foreigner," French, in his twenties, but has "mixed" in Chengdu for six or seven years. He seems to do nothing but love to soak in the teahouse, and like our tea drinkers, specifically looking for such dilapidated places as Broad Alley to drink tea. It was said that he rented a house near the Jiuyan Bridge Shuijingfang just because there were several teahouses opened in the residential area. But it is said that now he is sitting in Broad Alley to drink tea because the residence near the Shuijingfang has also been demolished.

I had work in hand today, so I didn't spend a long time with them. After only smoking two cigarettes and drinking half a bowl of tea, I rose, took my leave, and went to Qintai Road. On Qintai Road, I expected to visit two places, one called "Big Bar" and the other Sanhualou near Baihuatan Park. They all were the places I used to go for tea with my friends in the early years.

LEFT *An interior corner of Weiliu Teahouse.*

ABOVE *A night view of Dakejia Lane on Chunxi Road. Guanlan Pavilion, an old teahouse during the Republic of China, used to be on this street.*

However, the name of the "Big Bar" has been changed, and I don't like the layout and decoration there.

On the other hand, the Sanhualou is still the same as that in my memory. It is an empty wooden tower. I followed the spiral staircase from the bottom of the tower to the top, and took pictures while walking. There was no such pleasure when I only drank tea here before.

After coming out of the Sanhualou, I took a pedicab to Fanglin Road. In fact, going to Fanglin Road was just a bend along the Jinjiang River, and it took only about 10 minutes to walk there. I just thought the weather was so good, and it was more comfortable to take a pedicab. The bars on Fanglin Road were so famous that the road was called "Bar Street." The "Driftwood" bar I wrote about many times in the novel *The Witch Maker* was right on this street. But there were not many teahouses on this street. I came here for a teahouse called "Weiliu."

About Weiliu Teahouse, I wrote like this in an article: "There is a teahouse called 'Weiliu,' and I still don't understand what it means. But the building of the teahouse is small, exquisite, and antique, which was also described in one of my novels. A few days ago, just in this teahouse, I had tea with friends such as Jimu Langge, Li Yawei, Ma Song, Hua Qiu, Shi Guanghua, etc." The article's title is "Driftwood on Fanglin Road," mainly about bars and my drinking wine with Zhongmao and a group of friends at "Driftwood" before 2000. After the publication, a small story happened, and Zhongmao told me this:

"After this article was published, I received a call from an old friend I hadn't seen for a long time—so funny. Do you have a friend named He Xiaozhu?" "Yes."

(I thought, "What happened to Xiaozhu?") "He wrote an article in the *Evening News* about Fanglin Road, mentioning you, "Driftwood," and our "Weiliu," and said he doesn't understand its meaning." "What? Weiliu is run by you? I don't know it either." "It is run by six of our girlfriends. It means there are only six of us left."

"This, this, is more difficult to understand ..."

"Later, a friend said that Li Bai has a poem—'How many great men were forgotten through the ages? But great drinkers are more famous than sober sages.' Just hit it right."

"Yes, the meaning understood from Li Bai's poem is very good."

"Then you tell He Xiaozhu that we welcome you two to come here, and let's have fun together!"

"Okay, actually, I've been there a few times before, but I didn't know you were the boss. Let's have fun together later."

"OK, OK."

This article by Xiaozhu inadvertently made an old friend and me meet again.

My visit to "Weiliu" today just bore the meaning of helping my friend Zhongmao "visit" an old friend. When I looked around the teahouse with a camera like a spy, a woman came to me and said, "You can't take pictures casually here." I said, "The boss here is a friend of my friend." The woman smiled meaningfully and said, "Boss? Which one do you know?" I saw her demeanor and guessed that she was one of the six bosses in "Weiliu," so I asked her, "Do you know Zhongmao?" She said: "I don't know him." I thought maybe she was not the one Zhongmao recognized. I just said, "My friend Zhongmao knows one of your bosses. So, I come to take some pictures." I knew what I was saying was a little confusing, so I walked outside as I spoke, something like running away.

The big teapot faucet in front of Heming Teahouse.

The Shuijingfang dwellings loved by the Frenchman Li An are about to be replaced by new antique buildings, and there may also be teahouses, but as Li An said: "The feeling that once existed can't be found anymore."

I also went to Yongling. One of the two tea gardens had been demolished, and the other was no longer beautiful. Only a few old men and women were playing mahjong. I took a few photos but didn't ask for a cup of tea, so I left angrily in that I wasted a 10-yuan ticket with tea. Many years ago, I wrote a poem about drinking tea here, and recorded it here to express my nostalgia:

I saw water lilies planted in the pond
There was a man and a woman on the far side of the water lilies
I heard the sound of two tables of mahjong behind me
At that moment, it was raining
A man hurriedly ran down the path
I sat, but I was comfortable
Next to them are bamboo and willow trees
"Why don't the plants have sex with each other?"

I asked as I watched the rain fall even harder
A man and a woman took refuge in a house
And the mahjong player said, "Let's go, go"
And I, very comfortable
And remained seated
The whole garden is rarely occupied
The woman in the kiosk was reading a novel
I'm comfortable; it's indeed a wonderful feeling
And the plants swayed around
It was raining harder and harder, so I stood up
Let's go, let's go, that's what I said.

—"October 9 at Wang Jian's Tomb"

October 22, 2005

Old Chengdu during the Republic of China, co-authored by Wang Zehua and Wang He, was one of the reference books that I focused on reading when writing this book. A few days ago, I tried to follow the index in their book to see what the location of the old teahouses in the Republic of China looked like today. As a result, as I expected, most of the old teahouses were gone. In the past, the commercial circle formed by East Street, Chunxi Road, Commercial Market (Huaxing Street), and Gulou Street was also an area with dense teahouses. Today, this area is still the most prosperous commercial area in Chengdu, and there are still many teahouses. It's just that the old teahouses I was looking for couldn't be found anymore except Yuelai Tea Garden on Huaxing Street.

Today is Saturday. Every Saturday, from 2 p.m. to 5 p.m., Sichuan Opera excerpts are staged in Yuelai Tea Garden. The actors are all from the Chengdu Sichuan Opera House, and thus they are of professional performance level. Most fans are old fans, and their viewing standards should also be "professional." I don't have a special love for Sichuan Opera, but I do have a special feeling. When I was still playing the cello in a song and dance ensemble, I was borrowed by a county Sichuan Opera troupe to play in the band because the province was going to hold a Sichuan Opera performance. It was a modern repertoire, so the accompaniment asked for a cello to strengthen the band's bass. I lived with a group of Sichuan opera actors and musicians for half a year like this, so I naturally developed a special feeling for Sichuan opera. I have been in Chengdu for more than ten years, and I always said that I wanted to see Sichuan Opera once and often pass by the Sichuan Provincial Theater in Yanshikou. Still, the desire to see it never arises. Among my friends, Zhongmao understands Sichuan Opera, and it is said that he can still "play" on stage. We have also met a few times, but we only talked about it verbally and did not take any actual action. Maybe our current living conditions are not suitable for watching Sichuan opera in a teahouse so leisurely. Therefore, today is also an opportunity. My plan is not only to take a few photos at "Yuelai," but I want to spend this Saturday afternoon here and enjoy the Sichuan Opera.

Nearly a century ago, "Yuelai" was not only the leader of Chengdu teahouses, but also the "nest" of Sichuan Opera. It can be said that as a formed local drama, Sichuan Opera started from Yuelai Tea Garden. In the book *Old Chengdu during the Republic of China*, I read that there was no local opera in Sichuan before the Qing Dynasty. Sichuan Opera was fused and evolved from several local operas brought by immigrants from various provinces after the immigrants filled Sichuan in the early Qing Dynasty. At the end of the Qing Dynasty, Zhou Xiaohuai, the official of Quanye Dao,* found the drawbacks that hindered the development of Sichuan Opera: there were many troupes and no fixed performance venues; although there were many plays, the texts were not good, and prostitution and murderous plays were repeatedly banned. As a result, Zhou Xiaohuai implemented several measures: one was to build a new-style opera garden, which was now the Yuelai Tea Garden; the other was to set up an opera improvement committee, asking masters (bachelors, celebrities) to revise and create Sichuan Opera scripts, the most famous of which was *Love Detective* adapted by the imperial censor and poet Zhao Xi, Zhou Xiaohuai's teacher, in the late Qing Dynasty. This was also the earliest stereotyped script of the "Three Celebrations." "Three Celebrations" was an actors' group jointly established by artists from eight major opera troupes in the early 20th century, which was basically the "residence" theater group in Yuelai Tea Garden. Before this, the original scattered Sichuan opera genres could only stage one or two voices. After the "Three Celebrations," Kun, Gao,

---

*Editor's note: Quanye Dao here refers to the Sichuan Provincial Office of Industrial Promotion in the Qing Dynasty.

Hu, Dan, and Deng were able to be performed. As a result, Sichuan Opera has developed dramatically, and the performances in Yuelai Tea Garden have also experienced unprecedented prosperity.

At this time, the atmosphere was a little more open, and women were allowed to watch dramas, but they were separated from men by some barriers. Men entered from the main entrance of Huaxing Street, and women entered from the side entrance of Zitong Bridge. Men sat in the hall, and women sat on the balcony, in front of which were also curtains. Women "viewed the drama behind curtains." The seat under the balcony was the cheapest "ordinary seat," which was separated from the hall by a barbed wire. At the back of the hall, there was a "Danya seat," where more than ten soldiers from the police watched the play and maintained order. When the Danya team arrived and left, the band would play a welcome and farewell song ... It was unimaginable to watch a play without drinking tea, so a fixed wooden board was added behind the wooden chair, where a tea bowl could be put. Thus, drinking tea and watching the play would not be hindered by each other. The curtains upstairs were later removed, and the women could come on stage with a glittering appearance upstairs.

The show has begun. The theater was not quiet, but it was always noisy. Teenagers selling cigarettes, candy, peanuts, and melon seeds hung a wooden box on their chests, which contained their goods, and sold them in front of the audience. Square and steamy face masks would be scattered three to four times during a scene. If you didn't want it, the service staff would shout: "Yuelai's handkerchief, everyone has it!" Involuntarily, the face handkerchief flew out of his hand and landed on your face. In summer, there was also a "people-pulled fan," in which thin wooden boards were used to fix a row of multiple fans and then run through a long cable and pulled by people. There were eight such "fans" in the theater. The breeze was blowing in the theater, but the people pulling the fans were miserable.

Watching a play is a spiritual feast, not only in the play itself, but also outside the play. When a play was on, it was not impossible to see the glad eye on the stage and off the stage at the same time, although men and women were in separate seats. The young man in the hall wrote a note and asked a boy to send it to the female guest upstairs. The lady he liked looked at it and nodded with a smile, and they understood it. At the end of the play, the lady

The entrance to the "Wisteria Garden" of Jinjiang Hotel, which is called "Avoidance" by "witches."

The bamboo forests in Wangjianglou Park are still so dense and green.

Xue Tao Well in Wangjianglou Park. The old Chengdu teahouses used to fetch water here for brewing tea. This well was named after the poetess Xue Tao, so should the tea brewed with water from Xue Tao well be particularly fragrant?

walked out gracefully, and the young man was already waiting at the exit of the female guests on Zitong Bridge Street. The old mother serving female guests and the boys serving male guests were very awake in this regard. They knew the love story that happened in Yuelai Tea Garden … (*Old Chengdu during the Republic of China*)

In his book *Chengdu: Hibiscus Autumn Dream*, the poet Liushahe wrote like this:

(Yuelai Tea Garden) was a tea garden-type theater, completed in the first year of Xuantong (1909). In this tea garden-type theater, the stage was open on three sides and protruded forward. In the front pool, left pool, and right pool under the stage, tea tables were secretly arranged. A table was set with five chairs, which could seat five people. The tea table surrounded the stage on three sides, and the audience could watch the play from three sides. The price of the seats in the front pool was higher, and seats in the left pool and right pool were lower. Its pattern still retained the appearance of the tile and hook fence in the Song Dynasty. There were also different ones with floors above the front pool, left pool, and right pool, where female guests were seated exclusively to avoid confusion ... By the end of the 1940s, it was called "Yuelai Theater," and the performance *Blood Drop* was launched. *Nine Degrees of Wengong and Ten Degrees of Wife* was also staged by starring Chen Shufang, a large advertisement on the door, and an oil painting of a half-naked woman. A new play, *The Dumb Woman and the Lovely Wife*, was also staged, as something new in Sichuan Opera. At that time, Sichuan Opera was already in recession, showing that classical art had not fully adapted to the secular appetite of modern commercial society. At that time, I loved the new literature since the May Fourth Movement. I never watched Sichuan Opera, thinking it was too outdated. However, I secretly appreciated the singing of *Releasing Kui from the Stable*, *The Palace of Eternal Life*, and *Yanghetang*. Also, I liked to watch funny dramas such as *Marrying My Mother*, *Ask a Doctor*, and *The Tailor Stealing Cloth*.

Sitting in the Yuelai Tea Garden, recalling the old days described in the book, and then looking at the scene in front of me, I suddenly felt sad. All the good times could not be reproduced, neither the Sichuan Opera nor Yuelai Tea Garden. More than 90 percent of the people sitting in the tea garden were elders, just like the table behind me. From their conversation, I learned that they were not ordinary fans but retired Sichuan Opera actors. Today, they specially came to cheer for their acquaintances. When I sat down, I didn't know the rules for buying tea, so I got their warm guidance, which made me feel ashamed, because from their enthusiasm, I realized the meaning: there are still young people who come to see our Sichuan Opera, which is rare. Not only did the tea garden lose the noisy, lively, and eye-catching grand occasion described in the book, but the area and layout also shrunk greatly.

It was not divided into a hall and a floor like in "Yuelai" in the past, but it was truly like a tea garden, rather than a theater. The real theater was not here, but was another building outside the tea garden: Jinjiang Theater. There were still Sichuan Operas being staged there. I heard that they were mainly performed for foreign tourist groups. Of course, the plays and performances were also very authentic, but the ticket fare was not cheap. I took a look from the outside, and the price at the ticket office was 120–260 yuan. It was more than ten times the 15–20 yuan (with a bowl of tea) of Yuelai Tea Garden. In addition to the Jinjiang Theater, which used to occupy the Yuelai Tea Garden site, there were also several restaurants, such as "Dragon Chaoshou" with frontage facing the street. This spatial squeeze also reflected the current situation that the folk soil of Sichuan Opera has been seriously lost.

Some people say that Sichuan Opera is made in teahouses. Chengdu teahouses are prosperous, and it stands to reason that Sichuan Opera should also flourish. But unfortunately, that's not the case. I once worked in the Cultural Affairs Bureau and had some contact with the work of "revitalizing Sichuan Opera." There were many reasons for the downturn of Sichuan Opera, but one of the essential reasons has not been mentioned, that was, Sichuan Opera should not be "moved" out of the teahouse. It was like the fish leaving the water and the melon leaving the seedling. When Sichuan Opera left the teahouse, it lost its mass base.

Sichuan Opera is beautiful and elegant, but also popular and entertaining. Sichuan Operas that have entered the "temple" were either bluntly reduced to a tool for political propaganda, or could only be a "reserved program" for tourism. Between 1995 and 1996, the unrenovated Yuelai Tea Garden also had a "hot" scene, attracting thousands of tea guests and spectators. But what they watched was not the Sichuan Opera, but the "Casual Storytelling" by the folk artist Li Boqing. In those one or two years, Chengdu became fascinated by Mr. Li's "casualness" regardless of the class, because Mr. Li's "casual" style was different from the storytelling that had entered the "temple" before, in that his jokes and casual and natural performances have brought the art of storytelling back to the folk again. In other words, Mr. Li's success lies in the fact that he comes from the folk. He does not have the status of a cadre of national literary and art workers, but he has a life and talents tempered in it. Therefore, his "casual" style could move people. But unfortunately, the famous Teacher Li soon entered the "temple." As a cadre, it was difficult

Jinli, a newly built antique leisure street next to Wuhou Temple, is also a good place to drink tea and bask in the sun.

The red wall and tea sign flag of Du Fu Thatched Cottage.

for us to see him in the teahouse again. The "endangered" art of storytelling has not changed because of the appearance of Li Boqing. This case can also be used as circumstantial evidence for my discussion of the "cause" of the Sichuan Opera.

It's going too far, and let's come back. Today, Yuelai Tea Garden staged four folding operas: *Hong Ni Guan*, *Qin Yu*, *Three High-fives*, and *Jintai Jiang*. During the performance, the audience sometimes shouted and applauded. This was a true appreciation of the art of Sichuan Opera. I think, in front of such a "professional" audience, that kind of "Sichuan Opera vaudeville" with "Fast mask-changing" and "Spitting fire" would not have a market. I also went to the music pool in the side curtain to watch the show for half a day because of the "meet" I had with Sichuan Opera, as mentioned earlier. Both the drummer who was in charge of the drums and the piano player didn't interfere with my photo taking. I took a few extra glances at a girl who played the erhu because I had also played the erhu for many years in the song and dance troupe. At first, I did not dare to use the flash for being afraid to disturb them. But when I saw that the film was a bit "dull," I had the guts to use the flash, and I was still not interfered with. I thought this was the place that I liked and could produce a sense of intimacy.

Walking out of the Yuelai Tea Garden, I looked up at the sky. The sun I expected did not come out, but it started to rain in Chengdu style.

October 24, 2005

I went to bed after 5 a.m., but woke up before 12 o'clock. I think the sun outside the window woke me up. The brightness of the sun really surprised me, and the feeling of joy offset the sleepiness, so I quickly got up, scribbled in the shower, took the camera, and ran out, for fear that the sun would be gone in a while. I was going to visit Bacon Road today.

The name "Bacon Road" was very foreign, but the actual Bacon Road was not foreign at all. It was a typical Chengdu residential-like narrow street that was narrower than the Narrow Alley. Both sides of the street had low wooden houses, and the degree of "dilapidation" was no less than that of the Broad and Narrow Alleys before they were repaired. But even on such a street, there were teahouses and bars next to each other, with no gaps at all. Teahouses and bars were not so separate in function. Generally speaking, a teahouse was a teahouse during the day and a bar at night. Most of the people who come here for tea and bars are students. Because behind the small street was Sichuan University. After graduation, these students would not forget Bacon Road for several years, so they still come back for tea and bars, not only by themselves, but with old classmates and new friends. Therefore, Bacon Road has gradually become a gathering place for a group of white-collar workers and young artists. It could also be said that it was the birthplace of the earliest "petty bourgeoisie" in Chengdu, because only the "petty bourgeoisie" like to find such a feeling. Just like they later liked to go to the Broad and Narrow Alleys, Bacon Road was also a place for them to find feelings. The novel *Beautiful Ladies in Chengdu* has an interesting plot about Bacon Road, and the author of the novel, Wendi, is a frequent visitor to Bacon Road.

Of course, I'm talking about the Bacon Road of a few years ago. Now, there is no Bacon Road. Those wood-tiled houses and those "base areas" where the "petty bourgeoisie" drank tea and went to bars have been "removed"

Hibiscus floating in Huanhua Creek. Legend has it that Xue Tao, a poetess in the Tang Dynasty, often used hibiscus bark as raw material, and added hibiscus flower juice to make dark red exquisite small colored paper for writing poems and replies in Huanhua Creek in her spare time. The water in Huanhua Creek is clear and smooth, and the paper made from it is smooth and lovely, which is superior to other places. Therefore, the colored paper is known as "Huanhua paper."

like garbage, and replaced by modern buildings, as well as shopping malls and restaurants in modern buildings. And the new leisure community under construction is actually called "Bacon Road Promenade." In concept, it seems to build a "petty bourgeoisie" real estate somewhat related to the past. However, the real "petty bourgeoisie," I think, disdain such a "corridor." In their eyes, this "bacon" is not that "bacon."

In 1998, when I was working on the weekly magazine *On and Off the Screen*, I made friends with a group of Chengdu media, and began to haunt Bacon Road under their guidance. However, I was not a regular visitor there after all. I went there just for this group of new friends, and I didn't have the same special experience on this road as these friends have, so I didn't have that "nostalgia." Speaking of the year from 1992 to 1995, I rented a house in Zhulin Village on the other side of Sichuan University. Every day I went to work on Hongmen Street, and I had to pass through the intersection here. But I didn't know there was a Bacon Road inside the intersection. Presumably, my friends were sitting there drinking tea at that time, because it happened to be when they were studying at university. It's really a place for everyone to have their youth. Later, I saw an article about Bacon Road written by Simon Mei, another frequent visitor to Bacon Road:

The most prosperous period of Bacon Road was actually in the last ten years. In these ten years, bars, bookstores, and snack bars had been opened here, but most of them were teahouses. The open-air teahouses here were prosperous ... some were along the street, and some were family-style in small courtyards. No matter the season and weather, the day and night here were lively. I saw a book that introduced Tibet travel, and Chengdu was originally just a small chapter in it. When I turned to the chapter on Chengdu, it mentioned that one should go to Bacon Road for tea and snacks in Chengdu. Based on this, I could conclude that the author had really experienced Chengdu. Bacon Road is folk, and its leisure is hard to be understood by outsiders. You'd better not buy some of the officially designated snacks in the city center because very few still retain authentic deliciousness.

Bacon Road was even more important to our group of friends because it was once our living room and study room. We were here when we were reading books, watching football games, meeting with friends every week, and when entertaining friends from out of town. We had three friends known as "the three addicts of Bacon Road" who chased girls here. Some of our friends had a poetry club called "Happiness Troupe," and here was their base where they always held their activities. Those of us who wrote columns always heard interesting stories among friends here, and turned these into columns, and thus the name "Bacon Road" appeared in many media accordingly. When friends from other places come here, they always feel that they have found Chengdu in their expectations.

Now Bacon Road is left with rubble and has become a large enclosed garbage dump. A small house is standing here, and we are sitting here drinking tea now (excerpt from *The Last Autumn on Bacon Road*).

What a beautiful youth. Therefore, when I heard that Bacon Road was going to be demolished, I could understand the loss and sentimentality of Wendi and Ximen Mei. Although I had only been there for two or three years, when I went there with my camera today and found that the old sights could never be found again, I felt so sad that the bright sunshine in that empty intersection looked like a dream.

Nostalgia is in human nature. Nostalgia is also a kind of poetry. Although it was not their youth that I "lost" here, the past events soaked in tea and wine suddenly had no material relics to rely on, and it was difficult not to be "petty bourgeois." Thus, I immediately turned to the audio and video store still on the road outside the intersection, and bought more than ten DVDs that I wanted but did not buy, three of which were early Hollywood black-and-white detective films.

Taking pictures in the sun is exciting. I even felt that today's Chengdu was like Lhasa. Aiming at any place on the street, pressing the shutter at will, you would have all that could be called "works of art." I also thought that today's weather was perfect for Chengdu people to drink tea. So, I grabbed my camera and hurried to a few places: Wangjianglou Park, Wuhou Temple, Du Fu Thatched Cottage, and Huanhuaxi Park. The open-air cafes in these places were simply a sea of people. Especially when I arrived at Huanhuaxi Park, it was the time when the sun was about to set in the west, and the light was

The interior view of Heming Teahouse.

particularly charming. The Huanhuaxi photographed in this light was like going back decades or even hundreds of years ago. At that time, the water of the Huanhua stream was as clear and soft as the stream in the photo beautified by the sunset today, as if it could be directly used to make tea.

5

Mahjong Cannot Be Missed

Mahjong and teahouses have blended in complete harmony. It is difficult to tell whether mahjong relies on teahouses or teahouses rely on mahjong.

If there were no mahjong, would the teahouse still be so prosperous? Although mahjong does not account for the longevity of Chengdu teahouses, its importance cannot be doubted. Therefore, when writing about a teahouse, we have to talk about mahjong.

A widely circulated joke is that after the plane enters the sky over Chengdu, the stewardess asks the passengers, "Do you hear anything now?" The passengers answer in unison, "Yes, the sound of mahjong." "That is to say, dear passengers and friends, the plane is about to land in Chengdu. Please take the dice you carry with you."

The first time I heard this joke was from the old S. Old S is not only the old Chengdu, but also the old mahjong. He said that in the 1970s, mahjong still belonged to "FCR" (Feudalism, Capitalism, and Revisionism) and was banned. But just as there was "underground poetry" in that era, there was also "underground mahjong."

At that time in Chengdu, a woman named "Grannie Deng" was regarded as a grand master of Chengdu Mahjong. At a time when materials and spirits were scarce and barren, some young people were secretly introduced to learning mahjong from her. Old S himself probably learned to play mahjong in those secret years. The mahjong skills taught by Grannie Deng at that time were naturally very ancient. There must be dozens of points, including White Dragon, Green Dragon, East, South, West, North Wind, and Red Dragon. Old S spoke in awe of a kind of "celestial card," which was a type that exhausted almost all the points. Anyone who won this "celestial card" could make other people at the table go bankrupt. Therefore, the old S said the "celestial card" could not exist. That was to say, people who had the "celestial card" gave it up consciously because it was too full. Old S particularly admired the "deficiency" and "respect" in Chinese traditional culture.

How did Chengdu suddenly become the world-famous "Mahjong City"? Old S said that mahjong was a game imitating life. Various mechanisms of life can be reflected in mahjong. Chengdu people are moderate; in real life, they pay attention to being at ease with the situation and do not like taking risks. The virtuality of mahjong can be regarded as a complement, that is, to transfer all kinds of life fantasies to this virtual world to experience and play. Mahjong is also a very time-consuming game. The Chengdu Plain has always had good weather, and there are few natural and artificial disasters, so there was no worry about now and then, and there was much time to worry about. Playing mahjong is a good way to kill time. There were more deep-seated reasons, but it sounded like a cloud of fog, and I had to ignore it here.

In short, Old S was the first person among my friends who was proficient in "mahjong culture," and his skills were naturally first-class. Those who had played mahjong with him said he was good at mahjong. Some people encouraged Old S to stop doing business and make a living with mahjong. With his fantastic skills, there was no problem at all. Old S accepted this, really abandoned his business, and began going out and about on various mahjong occasions as a professional mahjong player.

The support of Chengdu teahouses is indispensable to the prosperity of Chengdu Mahjong. If there were no such developed teahouse culture, I am afraid it would not be possible to create the momentum of today's "Mahjong City." Of course, since things have developed up to the present, mahjong and teahouses have been blended in complete harmony. It is difficult to tell whether mahjong relies on teahouses or teahouses rely on mahjong. The current situation is that if you want to run a teahouse, you have to have a corner for people to play mahjong. Or, if you are going to start a mahjong game, you must run a teahouse. In a word, it is a complementary relationship.

Old S's mahjong campaign started from the Daci Temple. Daci Temple used to be a Buddhist temple, which was said to be very prosperous. It was later requisitioned by the Municipal Museum. Except for the office in this old building, the rest of the open space had been turned into a place to drink tea. Chengdu people, especially Chengdu culturati, like to drink tea at the Daci Temple. One was because of its proximity (the leading cultural institutions in Chengdu, such as the Federation of Literary and Art Circles, the Writers Association, the Radio Station, and several principal newspaper offices near the Daci Temple). The other was that the architectural features here were very consistent with the nostalgic mentality of culturati. At the same time, every open-air courtyard was shaded by ancient trees and the fragrance of birds and flowers. In such an environment, one would live a fairy life by drinking some rough tea and playing mahjong. Old S was a businessman, but he also wrote poems earlier, so people in Chengdu cultural circles recognized him greatly. Taking these "culturati" to try out the knife first was Old S's strategy when choosing Daci Temple as the first stop in his

The "pretty girls" playing mahjong in the tea garden.

The middle-aged and elderly people playing mahjong in the tea garden.

mahjong life. Because these culturati didn't have much money, they often played with little money and would not lose much. Old S had been soaking here for nearly half a year, and no one would fight him again. The reason was that although the culturati thought it was a small gamble, it was not a good feeling always to be a rabbit that has been cut. Old S, equipped with much better skills, won every game, so he naturally became a disgusting person disliked by others. In addition, Old S talked a lot, and he liked to talk about things at the poker table, and his words were harsh and mean, occupying the right to speak everywhere, which made the losers even more upset.

Helpless, Old S had to go elsewhere. Moreover, after this half-year experiment, Old S had enough confidence to win big money at this time.

He reconnected with those business partners in the past, gathered in a certain teahouse in Ximen. They played for several days and nights, all night long, winning and losing tens of thousands. Tea buildings only emerged in Chengdu in the early 1990s. Different from the traditional teahouses, the tea buildings were luxuriously decorated, with heating and cooling air-conditioning, where people could stay all year round; the facilities and services were also more comprehensive than the traditional teahouses. When you were sleepy, you had private rooms to sleep in, and when you were hungry, you could have all kinds of fried vegetables and snacks to satisfy your stomach; there was also a sauna health care, a hot bath, and a massage, which was very useful for poker players who had been sitting there all day. Most people who went to the tea building to play mahjong were "individual" business people. They stayed in the tea building, and both mahjong and work would not be delayed. Putting a mobile phone in the bag was equivalent to moving the entire company to the tea building.

Old S was naturally a victorious general on this occasion. However, according to Old S's own words, all wins were theoretical numbers. Since they were old friends in the business field for many years, it was inconvenient for Old S to refuse if they lost money and owed it them. Often, if one was defeated, disappeared, and never showed up again, the debt would become a debt forever. Although Old S had no problem making a living in this battle, he did not become as rich as people imagined. If the money won on the poker table was seriously pursued, a person with a temperament like Old S couldn't afford this shame anyway. Basically, this occasion was later broken up by Old S himself.

Next, the famous Old S could only fight guerrillas everywhere. That was to say, by going in and out of various mahjong occasions temporarily, he won some money quickly when people didn't know him very well. Once he was known, he would end up being alone in playing mahjong again and having to be forced to move and open up a new battlefield. Finally, after sighing, "the hero is lonely," on a winter day at the turn of the century, Old S officially gave up his mahjong business, and resumed his old trade of buying and selling clothes.

The mahjong game in Chengdu has changed since it was "opened." At the beginning of its "recovery," it was natural to play the kind of "old mahjong" taught by Grannie Deng with many points and high technology content. But this is a "fast" era. Although people don't care about the time spent sitting at the poker table all day, it is still unbearable to sit for half a day and win once. After all, the new rhythm of life has also changed people's mentality, and they value the results far more than the process. As a result, the Chongqing people first invented the "pull win," that is, they don't count any points, and when it's pulled together (Sichuan people often call it "Xia Jiao") it's called a win. "Pull win" is very fast, and there is no technical content. It is about strength (chips) and luck. Chengdu people quickly accepted "Chongqing Mahjong." But just like Chengdu accepting Chongqing hot pot, while accepting it, they always do not forget to transform it and make some moves. Compared with people in Chongqing, Chengdu people are gentler in temperament and have a slower sense of time. People in Chengdu feel that it is not gentle enough and too hasty to "pull win," which is not so enjoyable. Therefore, based on "pull win" of Chongqing Mahjong, Chengdu people invent "lacking suits," that is, except that the White, Green, and Red Dragon together with East, South, West, and North Wind must be removed, only when one of the three suits—the Dot, Bamboo, and Character are lacking, could one be qualified for the win; then, in order not to completely "break" the "tradition," several cards such as "pure one suit," "pairs" and "gongs" are left behind, which increases the interest in the game and appropriately expands the space for winning and losing, and also leaves some room for the display of mahjong skills. "Lacking suits" has thus become the main feature of "Chengdu Mahjong," which differs from that of "Chongqing Mahjong." Turning complex into simple, from simplicity to complexity, seems to have become a law of historical development just as long-term integration must be divided, and long-term

The chef of a restaurant watching people playing mahjong.

separation must be combined. After the basic "principle" of "lacking suits" was determined, in the past ten years, "Chengdu Mahjong" has also changed from time to time, and its changes have shown a trend of "from simplicity to complexity."

The first one is "singing and dancing." The so-called "singing and dancing" means that after "Xia Jiao," the fight is made clear, and no winning by one's own draw means no win. Of course, in this way, others will not "release the one that is just needed by others," and there will be fewer chances of winning. But if there is a win, there will be double points. As for why it is called "singing and dancing," it probably means "calling and fighting" (that is, I will win with that card). Then there is soon a "blood battle to the end." The gameplay of "blood battle to the end" is that if one player wins, he leaves first, and the other three players continue to play; if another one wins, he leaves, and the remaining two players continue to play until one of them wins. This is "blood battle to the end," a very vivid name. One or two persons can be invited to the original four persons to form a five-player battle or a six-player battle. In this game, it is very tragic to lose when you are out of luck. If one is usually an expert in releasing the one that is just needed by others, it is very likely for him to release that one in a round by himself. I don't know how to play the "river of blood" that appeared after that. However, listening to that name, you know you will need a strong will to afford it.

I've been thinking about several questions, very wonderful questions, and that is:

- Be it "pull win," "lacking suits," "blood battle to the end," or "river of blood," who actually developed the rules of mahjong first?
- It is almost the case that everyone in the city plays according to these rules when a certain kind of rule appears. And we know the reality is that we

don't have an organization like the "Mahjong Association" issuing official documents about the game's rules, let alone promoting it on the public media. Then, how does one achieve this consistent "compliance" with the rules?

- How can something similar to the "convention" that happened to mahjong spread so efficiently without resorting to modern means of communication (including administrative orders)? Once it spreads, how can a "consensus" be reached in the crowd so smoothly?
- Are there any rules for winning or losing in mahjong? Are there any similarities between the principles of the game and the securities market? And if so, what are the differences?
- What role does mahjong play in the economic life of a city? What are its marginal effects?

I don't think these questions are mysteries as long as it's studied and treated as a serious matter. At least, we should put aside the generalization of the so-called "mahjong culture" just like the "teahouse culture," and start to open up a new project or science about "mahjong" (let's name it temporarily) with a scientific attitude and means.

For my part, driven by curiosity, I can ask such questions. But to study these issues is far beyond my ability. "Mahjong" science should probably be an academic field in which economists, sociologists, and even political scientists should be involved individually or jointly. What I can do is still limited to the observation and research on the form and mentality of various people in the mahjong game.

Mr. B is another old friend of mine. He played mahjong relatively late, but now is crazier than anyone else. He had never touched mahjong before he was 30 years old, but he found it fun after he did. He also regretted it was too late to find it, and was crazy about finally going on the "last train." In the past few years, half of the money he earned in business may have contributed to his "mahjong" friends, because his hemp friends have openly and affectionately referred to him as "our cash machine." However, he still enjoyed it. He didn't care how much he lost, but he just enjoyed the one time he won. It was challenging for him to win once, so as long as he won, he must treat the guests to celebrate. I have asked other friends, what happened to Mr. B? Wouldn't it be you who united to "fool" him? Friends flatly denied it, saying that they were all friends; how could it be? It was he who was too dippy.

Speaking of Mr. B's dippy nature, I believed it. I never quite understood what he was saying. That was to say, when he spoke in a daze, he was clever, wise, and quite funny. However, once he tried to speak logically, I couldn't understand it. Therefore, in the more than ten years of getting along with Mr. B, I have never cooperated with him in any serious business, but just drank and talked nonsense. I was also worried when he got hooked on mahjong. How could he count? The fact was also true. People who have watched him play said that he often could not find he would win in advance and often destroyed the coming "win." Sometimes he even didn't know he had already won. He was fortunate to win money occasionally. For example, the "win" card he has knocked out could still be drawn back after two laps; after two more laps, he drew another card and won by his own draw. The people watching next to him were amazed, saying there was no way to prevent this lunatic from winning money.

Winning treats was one of the happiest things for Mr. B. After winning two or three hundred yuan, he would spend five or six hundred yuan on treats. But he felt happy to do it.

People say that a person's character can be seen at the poker table, and that's true.

Brother Lei was recognized as a smart man. When we were hanging out together, he was very fond of chasing girls, and scheming. Every time he chased the girl, he had a plan in advance. He liked to have a plan for everything, and love was no exception. We were often involved in his "prewar" planning at that time. For example, when it was popular to study English, he would go on a date with an English book, and then, at an inadvertent time (actually intentional), the English book fell out of his pocket. Or, when asking a girl to come home, he would put the end game of weiqi on the table beforehand; when he learned that the girl was going upstairs, he would open the door ahead of time and then focus on holding a large brush on the table, wielding the brush on rice paper. Also, pretending to be lost was also his old routine. He suddenly disappeared when the other party had already developed a good impression of him. In fact, he hadn't gone far and had been lurking near the girl, observing whether she felt pain because of his leaving without saying goodbye. He was a liar and a liar addict. For example, he would casually tell the girl that some singer was his buddy, and they had dinner together yesterday. When happy, he would improvise and say he was currently working as an assistant for director XX, looking for actresses. These tricks worked a decade ago, but they don't work anymore. We once asked Brother Lei, do you really love this girl? Brother Lei was aggrieved and said angrily, why don't I love her? If I didn't love her, would I spend so much effort? He also blamed us, "you always think badly of me, while in fact, I'm not half as bad as you were." We said, "if you are sincere, you should treat her with sincerity. What are you doing with so many tricks?" Brother Lei said, "You don't understand. Love is an art! Is love without artistic content still called love? It can just be called sleeping." So we knew that love was an art, and Brother Lei has always been a "youth" who loved art from the past to the present.

When smart Brother Lei, "Art Youth," went to the mahjong table, he would, of course, use his smart artistic talents. He liked to build "box cards" the most. The so-called "box card" was to stack the cards of the same color together intentionally when shuffling them, allowing him to take advantage of the cards when they were drawn. Speaking of the stacking "box," it was really a skill (it is an exaggeration to say that it is art), and it took some effort. Because before drawing cards, the dice must be rolled, and the number of points on the dice determines which direction to start drawing cards from. The probability of getting the "box" you built depends on the dice. This requires that after you build the "box," you must be able to roll the dice and control the number of points you need. It is not something that can be practiced in a short period of time. That is to say, the key to building "boxes" is not building "boxes," but rolling dice.

Brother Lei was so bright, and he, of course, thought of this. He practiced rolling dice hard at home. In the early years, people only threw one dice at the poker table. Later, maybe everyone noticed the problem of building "boxes" and asked to roll two dice at once. Brother Lei's skill in throwing one dice was already somewhat skilled. Not to mention nine out of ten, there were three out of four. With this 30 to 40 percent chance of winning, the probability of winning was relatively high. However, the two dice stumped Brother Lei, and he couldn't use two dice to roll the number he wanted. But he was unwilling to give up the fun of building "boxes." As a result, the "boxes" he made were often caught in other's hands to achieve one pure suit. Later on, the fashionable "machine mahjong" (a mahjong table that can automatically shuffle the mahjong tiles by machine) appeared, so there was no chance to build a "box" anymore.

But that wouldn't make Brother Lei feel at ease and play cards honestly. He started stealing cards. That was, when shuffling the cards, when other people were not paying attention, he would draw two more cards and hide them in the palm of his hand without attracting people's attention. Then, when appropriate, he would replace unwanted cards to increase his chances of "winning." This was a perilous move, the risk factor of which was no less than that of being a special agent. Therefore, Brother Lei was often nervous at the poker table. No matter how cold the weather was, some sweat was always coming out of his forehead.

In addition to these "illegal" calculations, within the scope of legality, he was also fond of complexity instead of simple things. He was not good at math, but he desperately developed his math half-brain for mahjong. He practiced the skill of memorizing cards. That was, he remembered what cards were released one by one in his mind, and then analyzed the cards in the hands of each party and what cards were left untouched on the table. And from this, it could be judged who would win next and which card they need now. If he happened to have this card in his hand, he would hold it tightly and never release it, which was to "hinder cards."

These calculations were generally correct, and people who play cards a lot do have to have some basic skills in memorizing and "guessing" (analyzing cards). However, our brother Lei took this too far, and thought he was a math genius and believed in his own judgment. Therefore, he often removed the "close-by cards" (the cards that are next to each other) and discarded them because he did not want others to make two pairs, or he thought that he had "guessed" which card others needed. According to the rules of the game, "checking" at the end of the mahjong game will usually be carried out, commonly known as "checking household registration." That is to say, if at the end of the game, no one wins, then the game is considered "yellow," but if you do not have "flower tiles," you will pay damage to the other three sides. Usually, when there was no "winning" in advance, some people deliberately discarded the tiles at the end, because they would rather pay damage for one than three. But when Brother Lei came to such a critical time, he was not able to discard a tile successfully because others didn't want the cards he thought were crucial at all.

But people still said enthusiastically that Brother Lei played well. He also thought so in that there was no problem with this way, mainly because he was out of luck.

I am not a mahjong player, but I don't feel uncomfortable living in "Mahjong City" either. Over the years, I've gotten used to hearing the sound of mahjong everywhere I went. Even just outside the city, in farmhouses (the leisure venues run by farmers to eat, drink tea and play mahjong in their own courtyards), resorts, scenic spots, cruise ships, and other places, all the people I encountered were mahjong players. The so-called going out to play in the eyes of the Chengdu people is to play mahjong in another place; although they head for scenic spots and historical sites, they are not really going to play in the mountains and waters. I had observed that when people sat together without playing mahjong, they seemed to have nothing to say. In the past, there was nothing to talk about. When friends or family gathered together, they just watched TV silently. Nowadays, fewer people watch TV, and more people enjoy playing mahjong. Even when traveling abroad, some people just find a hotel, sit and play mahjong together. After playing day and night for a few days, the tour is over, and they return home, indicating that they have been to Paris and Bangkok. The topic, with family and friends after coming back, is still about mahjong—I once had a chance to make "seven pairs," but I discarded the wrong card.

In Chengdu, two other occasions are the paradise for playing mahjong: a wedding and a funeral. Funerals, in particular, are often called "Da Sanghuo," which is busier than the mahjong at wedding, because, according to the custom in Chengdu, the dead will be placed there for three days after they pass away. After being placed there for three days, the body will then be taken out for cremation with a farewell ceremony.

Those involved in the "Da Sanghuo" are generally relatives, friends, and neighbors. Several pergolas are set up in an open space in the residential area. Under the pergola, except for a place used to set up a mourning hall, the rest of the space is filled with mahjong tables. The funeral company not only provides materials and services for erecting tents and arranging mourning halls, but also prepares mahjong tables and mahjong for customers. The family of the deceased should keep vigil beside the coffin. The so-called vigil-keeping means playing mahjong with relatives and friends. Some friends from Beijing were very confused about this, and not used to it. They thought that such a cheerful atmosphere lacked due solemnity for the parting person. In fact, they did not understand that this was the difference between the cultures of the North and the South. In the Bashu culture, there is a saying of "red and white happy events." A wedding is a happy event, and the representative color is red; a funeral is also a happy event, and the representative color is white. Therefore, playing mahjong during the funeral is naturally appropriate. It seems to be somewhat related to the allusion to Zhuangzi's "beating the basin and singing," meaning "face death with a positive attitude."

Among them, some people were neither relatives, friends, nor neighbors of the deceased. They were a group of "professional members" specializing in "Da Sanghua." Wherever there were "funerals," they were there with a very professional looking. The host was not disgusted with these people either. "All the people who come here are guests." If these people go to other places, they would have to pay for their meals after playing mahjong. While at a funeral, the host's family had to take care of the lunch and tea. No matter whether one wins or loses, one would have a boxed lunch and flower tea, so why not do it?

Regarding "Da Sanghuo," the government had explicitly banned it for a while, but didn't take it seriously, so this custom has still been thriving as ever.

However, considering that the scene of government officials playing mahjong in the teahouse near the office during working hours was prevalent, which greatly affected the government's image, it was also banned by issuing a document. The business of some teahouses also experienced a slump for a while. It was also seen in the newspaper that some civil servants were dismissed for playing mahjong, which played the role of a warning to the people next to them. I went out with a few civil servants once, and indeed we did not play mahjong. But not playing mahjong was also troublesome in that we had nothing to say sitting with each other. It's no wonder because we were so familiar with each other, and we had already said what we should say. What else was there to say? And it was not fashionable to collide with sparks of thought. Besides, it's not easy for everyone to get along with life. It sounds reasonable to have some entertainment to temporarily escape from reality and relieve the inner pressure.

I had a friend who was an official in government. He seemed to have foresight, becoming obsessed with fishing before mahjong was banned. Therefore, he didn't feel uncomfortable with "forbidding mahjong" at all, although he was also a "mahjong fan." When free, he enjoyed driving a car to find fish ponds or reservoirs for fishing. On the other hand, those unprepared buddies would feel a little anxious all day long in their spare time.

By the way, when the "forbidding mahjong" first started, business in Chengdu teahouses was obviously depressed for a while. Fortunately, in the past two years, "Fighting the Landlords" (a poker game) has become popular in Chengdu again. No matter which teahouse you go to, you could see many people playing "Fighting against the Landlords," for which another vigorous "renaissance" was ushered in the business of the teahouse.

The decorated archway of Heming Teahouse.

6

Tea on the Peak of Mount Meng

There are stone flowers on the peak of Mount Meng in Jiannan, some with small squares or scattered buds, which rank number one.

—Li Zhao, *Supplement to the History of the Tang Kingdom*

The water in the middle of the Yangtze River,
the tea on the peak of Mount Meng.

—Adapted from Li Dezai,
"Zhonglu · Yangchun Song · Zeng Cha Si"

During these days of visiting Chengdu teahouses, a mountain has always appeared in my mind: the famous Mengding Mountain.

The tea history data before the Six Dynasties (AD 222–589) shows that the tea industry in China first started in Shu. Shu is the cradle of Chinese tea culture, and its specific location is Meng Mountain in Mingshan County (now Mingshan District), Ya'an, Sichuan, which is what we usually call Mengding Mountain.

According to legend, in the Western Han Dynasty (202–8 BC), a medicinal farmer named Wu Lizhen discovered the medicinal properties of wild tea in Mengding Mountain, so he transplanted seven tea trees for the first time to a forest clearing. He was said to be the first person in the world to cultivate domesticated tea trees. From the first year of Emperor Xuanzong's Tianbao in the Tang Dynasty (742), Mengding Mountain Tea had been listed as a

The tea garden on Mengding Mountain.   *The open-air tea garden in Tiangai Temple of Meng Mountain.*

special tribute tea for the central court to worship ancestors and emperors. The history of "Mengshan Gong Tea" lasted more than 1,000 years till the end of the Qing Dynasty. "Mengding Tea" was the general name for all kinds of famous teas in Meng Mountain, which included five famous traditional tea such as Ganlu, Yellow Buds, Stone Flower, Wanchun Silver Leaf, and Jade Leaf Changchun, together with the special-grade green teas created later, hot air fixation and stir fixation tea at all levels, various jasmine teas, Tuo tea, South Roadside tea, etc. These teas are now widely included in the "tea list" of Chengdu teahouses.

The first time I went to Mengding Mountain was in the summer of 1991. At that time, I didn't pay much attention to the monuments on the mountain, but the climate of Mengding Mountain deeply touched me. It was cloudy for a while, and sunny for a while; it was still sunny just now, but in a blink of an eye, it was shrouded in fog and drizzle. Knowledgeable people told me that "Mengding Tea" enjoyed an enduring reputation due not only to human factors (from picking, production, blending, packaging, etc., all links are meticulous), but also to its unique nature. The annual average temperature in the mountains is 14.5°C, and the annual precipitation is 2000–2200 mm, forming an ecological environment with drizzle and clouds all year round. Such a natural climate can weaken direct sunlight and increase scattered light, which is very beneficial to the growth and development of tea trees and the synthesis of aromatic substances. Ancient books recorded: "Mount Meng is covered by the sky, and the essence is nourished." "Many beautiful ridges on the top of Mount Meng do not produce evil grass but fine tea leaves."

I've been waiting for a good day to go up to Mount Meng.

On October 25, 2005, the weather in Chengdu was fine, and I thought the climate of Mengding Mountain would not be bad. I hurriedly packed up and went straight to Xinnanmen Bus Station. My companion was my wife, An Ke. After about two hours drive, we arrived at Mingshan County (today's Mingshan District), known as the "Tea Capital." Then, we transferred to a small bus resembling a Changan van, winding up the mountain. It happened to be the off-season tourism after the "October Golden Week," and entering Mount Meng was like an uninhabited land. The Qingquan Villa, where we chose to stay, was next to the ropeway under the mountain gate, and we were the only two guests that day. Without the expected sun, the famous Mount Meng cloud and mist loomed among the trees around the villa. We were still hesitating about whether to go up the mountain today, or stay for one more night and wait for the sun to come out tomorrow before going up the mountain. The villa's owner told us that it was not predictable when the sun would come out. If you wanted to take pictures, we'd better go to the mountain today, but who knows, it might also be a rainy day tomorrow. The owner also suggested that we should not take the cable car; climbing up the mountain would be very comfortable. We did think so. It was rare to enter the mountain once, and we were charged 60 yuan per person for the entrance fee, but it was really not worthwhile if we didn't climb up the mountain. On the way up the mountain, I saw a farmer's inn which offered food and accommodation. In the courtyard, a table of people was drinking tea and playing mahjong. I began to regret living in the villa under the mountain gate. Had I known it earlier, I would have gone up the mountain to stay here, and it must have been much more "popular." We also stopped and talked for a while with a peasant woman selling tea by the roadside. We praised her hand-made insoles for being very beautiful and promised to buy some of her tea when coming back later. There were many temples on Mount Meng, and we didn't rest until we reached Tiangai Temple. There was a large group of people drinking tea and playing cards here. We also sat down at the outdoor cafe next to us and asked for two cups of tea. The ginkgo trees in Tiangai

Temple were so big that a camera couldn't even photograph them. Looking at the age of the trees marked on the trunks, you could see that each one was a thousand or two thousand years old. At this time, I recalled that in the summer of 1991, I sat here and tasted Mengding tea for the first time. We asked the girl selling tea in the tea garden whether it was the top there. The girl smiled and said it had only started here, and there were still many scenic spots in the back mountain. In fact, the tea garden that I wanted to shoot has already been filmed along the way, so I just wanted to finish my work and sit here drinking tea without moving. However, An Ke still had fun with it. At 4:30 in the afternoon, we continued climbing the rugged and steep mountain for about an hour. It was past 5:00 when we reached the Red Army Memorial Hall. The caretaker in the memorial hall told us that we just took a detour, and it only took 10 minutes to walk from another road. Surely enough, and unbelievably, it's so close to going down by taking that road to Tiangai Temple. Moreover, it also reminded me that I walked on this road in 1991, just that the road 14 years ago was not as good as it is today, and it can be seen that those stone stairs were only laid in the past year or two. The imperial tea garden and the ancient well on the way also reminded me of the pictures taken by my friends who went up the mountain with me.

The site of Gumeng Spring, which is separated from the Royal Tea Garden by a wall. According to legend, it is the place where Wu Lizhen planted tea and drew water, also known as "Dragon Well." The well is covered, and it will not overflow in the rain and will not dry up in the drought. There are two steles engraved with "Gumeng Spring" and "Meng Spring" beside it.

It really rained the next day. Also, the rain had been falling from the night before. From the balcony of the villa, the whole of Mount Meng was really a misty and rainy world. Fortunately, after accepting the owner's words, the photo-taking work was not delayed yesterday. We thanked her from the bottom of our hearts, and had no regrets about staying in her villa. Before going down the mountain, we also stopped by the Tea Culture Museum to have a look.

The museum was also next to the ropeway; its full name was "Chinese Tea Culture Museum." The tickets were 20 yuan per person. I first asked if I could take pictures of it. If it were permitted, I would go into it. I said I was writing a book about teahouses. The security guard at the gate said that it was not allowed to take pictures, but if you were writing a book, then just take pictures if you want. So, that day, not only did I take the photos I wanted, but I copied and excerpted from the museum and pieced together the following information on "Sichuan Tea."

Gu Yanwu, a scholar in the Qing Dynasty, investigated and researched tea in ancient China, and came to the following conclusion: "Since the State of Qin conquered the State of Shu, the drinking of tea emerged." He pointed out that the drinking of tea in various places gradually spread after the annexation of Bashu by the State of Qin. According to the *Record of Huayang State*, Sichuan tea was listed as a tribute in the time of King Wu of Zhou (about 1058 BC). In 59 BC, Wang Bao, in Western Han Dynasty, recorded in *Tong Yue*: "buying tea in Wuyang and purchasing lotus in Yang Pond," which reflected that in the Chengdu area at that time, tea drinking had become a fashion, and there were special tea sets. Due to the need for tea consumption, tea was commercialized. Tea markets such as Wuyang (now Pengshan District, Sichuan) also appeared. Zhang Zai, a native of the Western Jin Dynasty (AD 266–316), praised tea as "the superior" among various beverages in the poem *On Chengdu Baitu Tower*, with its flavor being famous all over the world. "Fragrant tea is clear and fresh, and its flavor spreads in places afar." In the Tang Dynasty, there were large-scale tea gardens in Sichuan, enjoying fame all over the country. According to historical records such as Lu Yu's *Tea Classic* and Li Zhao's *Supplement to the History of the Tang Kingdom* in the Tang Dynasty, there were about 50 kinds of famous teas, 18

The sculpture corridor about the Tea Art in Meng Mountain in the rain and fog reproduces the elegant "Eighteen Movements of the Dragon," the tea art of Mengdingshan School created in the Song Dynasty. It is said that the "Eighteen Movements of the Dragon" integrates tea ceremony, martial arts, dance, Zen, and Yi theory, and every move is an imitation of the movements of a dragon, which sounds very fantastic.

of which came from Sichuan, indicating the prosperity of the tea industry in Sichuan. Lu Yu praised Sichuan's Mengding Tea as the best tea in the world. Since the Tang and Song dynasties, Sichuan tea has been famous worldwide for Mengding Tea. In the Ming Dynasty, Wang Yue praised Mengding Tea as "the first tea in the world" in the poem "Mengshan Dolomite Tea."

In the past, when it was time to pick spring tea every year, local officials chose an auspicious day and led the village and monks to worship the gods, and then 12 tea-pickers (symbolizing 12 months of a year) picked tea in the "Imperial Tea Garden." Here, the tea-picking monks washed their hands and burnt incense. When picking tea, each person picked 30 buds, with 12 people picking a total of 360 tea buds (symbolizing one year). These picked imperial teas would be sent to an ancient place where monks made imperial tea—the Zhiju Temple. The tea would be processed and refined there. In the Zhiju Temple, monks made tea in the most traditional way. They used bamboo scissors to select tea leaves, then roasted and kneaded them into shape, cooled them down, baked them slowly over low heat, cooled them down again, put them in silver bottles, packed them in boxes which were sealed, and finally delivered them to the tea messenger to send to the imperial capital.

They would produce 28 *jin* of "Pei Gong" tea (meaning serve as a foil) only for the emperor to taste. The 28 *jin* of tribute tea were picked from the hundred acres of tea fields outside the "Imperial Tea Garden." In ancient times, because the emperor asked to drink the original Mengding Tea, several 16-year-old virgins, who had fasted for a month, were asked to pick off the buds one by one with their lips so as to avoid being destroyed by their nails and ensure the freshness of the sprouts. The picked buds were sent to the Zhiju Temple, where they were processed into "Pei Gong" Tea by the tea-making monks through multiple processes, and then sent to the imperial capital together with the "Zheng Gong" Tea (a formal tribute).

There was also a legend about the Zhiju Temple in Mengding Mountain, where tribute tea was made: there were two stone dragons in the temple. One was called "Dry Dragon," and the other was called "Wet Dragon." The dry dragon flutters ashes all year round. Whenever the rain blew, and the wind blew, there was no trace of water on it, while the wet dragon was the opposite. As a result, the common people regarded them as "sacred dragons," which became very popular throughout the year, and the "meteorological station" on Mengding Mountain in ancient times.

What surprised me the most was the famous "Ancient Tea Route," which, according to new research, actually originated in Mount Meng. This discovery undoubtedly excited the officials of Ya'an and Mingshan County (now Mingshan District). At the 8th International Tea Culture Symposium and the 1st Mengdingshan International Tea Culture Tourism Festival in 2004, they officially issued a "Declaration," saying Mengding Mountain was the "Holy Mountain of Tea Culture in the World" for the following reasons:

- Wu Lizhen, in the Western Han Dynasty, planted seven tea trees in Mengding Mountain, which was the first of its kind in artificial tea planting. From this, the world tea civilization was born, and the tea culture spread throughout China and abroad.
- From the Tang Dynasty to the Qing Dynasty, the tea picked before the Qingming Festival in the Mengding Imperial Tea Garden had always been the special tea for the central court to worship the sky and ancestors during the Qingming Festival.
- Chinese Zen has been integrated with tea since ancient times. Originating from the Song Dynasty, the *Mengshan Food Ritual* that has been recited so far was born in Yongxing Temple in Mengshan. In the *Buddhist Chanting Collection · Eight Praises*, "Mengshan Queshe Tea," which was produced in Mengding Mountain, was required to be used to worship Buddhas and Bodhisattvas.
- After the establishment of the Song Dynasty, the only remaining "Tea Horse Division" in the country was located in Xindian Town, Mingshan County (now Mingshan District), at the foot of Mengshan Mountain.

The "Ancient Tea Route," which stretched for thousands of miles, started from here, forming a "carrying culture" rich in national characteristics.

- Founded by Master Chan Hui in the Song Dynasty, the famous tea technique of Mengdingshan School in China, namely, "Eighteen Movements of the Dragon," Chinese Zen and tea technique, and the "Ancient Tea Route" tea technique, were forming a new tea culture industry.

Postscript

I contracted the manuscript of *Chengdu Teahouse: Half of the City's Dwellers Are Tea Drinkers* because the planner of the book did not require it to be an academic book to conduct a comprehensive study of the teahouse industry in Chengdu, but allowed it to be what I have seen and heard about Chengdu teahouses over the years from my perspective, which gave me the guts to write. But this is different from writing novels, after all, in that too much fiction is not acceptable. Although it cannot be said that the words and sentences are true and have their origins, basic facts cannot be violated. In addition to writing what I have experienced truthfully, I find the basis for those parts I have not experienced through the review of relevant materials in the process of writing. All directly cited materials in the book have the source indicated. Here, special thanks are due to Deng Muqing (deceased), Mr. Liushahe (deceased), Wang Zehua and Wang He, two ladies who are the authors of three books respectively: *Old Lores in Chengdu*, *Old Chengdu during the Republic of China*, and *Chengdu: Hibiscus Autumn Dream*. Thanks go to Mr. Xiao Ping and Mr. Wu Hong (deceased), who provided me with other references. I would also like to thank my friend Jiang Hai, who provided photos of the tea garden in the old Daci Temple that cannot be found anymore. And my thanks also go to many of my friends in Chengdu for their understanding and support during the two months I "retreated" to write this manuscript.

ABOUT THE AUTHOR

HE XIAOZHU, born in 1963, is a renowned poet and author hailing from the "Third Generation" avant-garde poetry movement and the "Non-Fei" school of poetry. His prolific body of work includes poetry collections, novels, and essays. He resides in Chongqing and Chengdu, where he writes and hosts the "Two Lighters" literary public website.